MW00979992

Christmas Love

God bless the master of this house,

the mistress, also,
And all the little children
that round the table go:
And all your kin and kinsfolk,
that dwell both far and near;
I wish you a Merry Christmas,

and a Happy New Year.

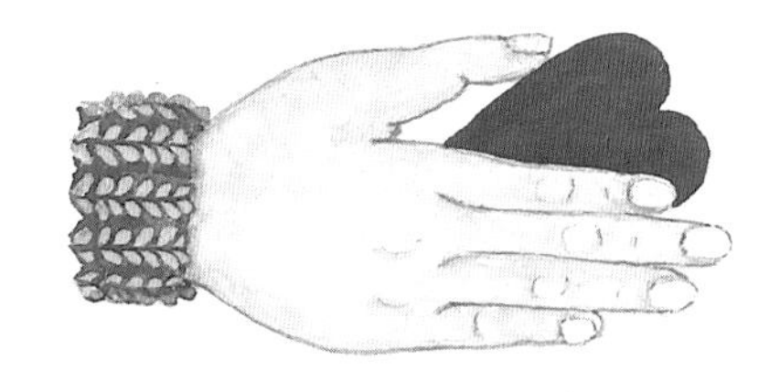

Christmas from the Heart of the Home

By Susan Branch

LB

Little, Brown & Company
Boston Toronto London

FIRST EDITION

Library of Congress Cataloging-in-Publication Data
Branch, Susan.
Christmas from the heart of the home.
Includes index.
1. Christmas cookery. 2. Entertaining. 3. Christmas decorations. I. Title.
TX739.2.C45B73 1990 641.5'68 90-6227
ISBN 0-316-10638-0

10 9 8 7 6

Published simultaneously in Canada by Little, Brown & Company (Canada) Limited

PRINTED IN HONG KONG

G' Grandpa comes to Christmas Dinner 1956

The girls in their leopard jammies Paula, Me, Shelly & Mary ~ 1963

Me, Jim, Chuck, Brad, Steve-Janie (my pal) & Mom
Decorating the tree 1958

DEDICATION

Our house at Christmas was so full of excitement and secrets, games and noise and love — growing up with these people was the best thing that ever happened to me. I wish them the merriest of Christmases everafter ♥.

Mary & Paula ~ Mom made the stockings ♥

The Tree ~ 1962

Dad & Grandma ♥ Christmas Kiss ♥

Six of us ~ Jim, Bradley, Paula, Me, Chuckie & Stephen 1956

"O WINTER, KING OF INTIMATE DELIGHTS . . .

CONTENTMENT

Fire-side enjoyments, home-born happiness,
And all the comforts that the lowly roof
Of undisturb'd retirement, and the hours
Of long uninterrupted ev'ning, know."

William Cowper

CONTENTS

APPETIZERS 9
Decking the Halls 22
NOGS & GROGS, PUNCH & TEA . 25
Snow Business & Snow Magic . . 34
Christmas Is for Children 37
SIDE DISHES 39
Stocking Stuffers 58
Recipe for a Happy Christmas . . 59
Christmas Caroling 60
The Fireplace 61
Christmas Day 62
MAIN DISHES 63
DESSERTS 79
Ideas for Collections 104
Baked Christmas Decorations . 105
BREAKFAST & BRUNCH . . 109
Christmas Superstitions . . . 110
INDEX 125

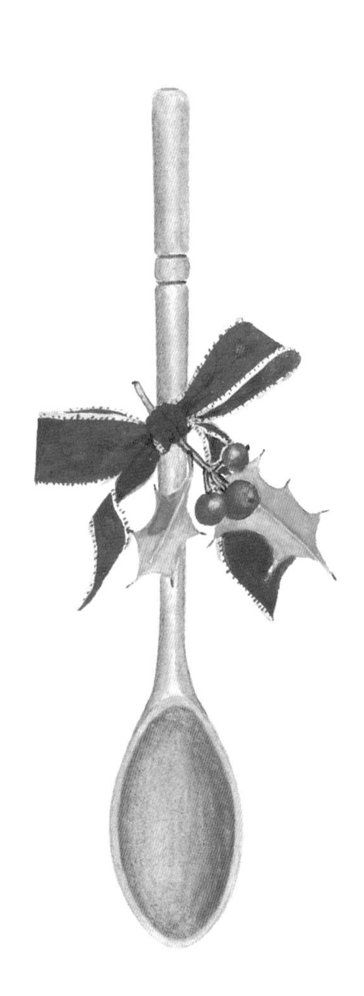

APPETIZERS

"I'm not going *anywhere* till I finish." ♥ Santa

CHRISTMAS LOVE ♥

Food, Family, & Friends — my three favorite things at Christmas. And when the family & friends show up, it's nice to have a selection of easy & quick recipes to put together — little "noshes." ♥ Here are some of my favorites:

It wouldn't be Christmas without the little plates of cookies, candies & nuts. Make tiny cakes in the shapes of hearts or stars — a plate of powdered sugar-dusted cookies in the shapes of stars & moons is especially pretty ♥.

Two kinds of spiced nuts:

1. 1/4 c. butter
   1/2 tsp. Tabasco sauce
   2 tsp. Worcestershire sauce
   1 Tbsp. garlic salt
   2 c. pecan halves

2. 1/4 c. butter
   1/4 c. chutney
   1 tsp. curry powder
   2 c. almonds

For each recipe: melt butter; stir in spices; coat nuts with mixture. Spread on cookie sheet & bake at 350° for 20-25 min., till brown, stirring occasionally — cool on brown paper (bag). ♥

Lobster Nancy: Butter a baking dish very well. Spread dry breadcrumbs over the bottom; top with cooked lobster meat. Bake in 350° oven till hot (don't overcook). Stir; serve with lemon wedges ♥.

Cold Shrimp: Boil peeled & deveined shrimp just till done. Arrange on a plate & serve with catsup mixed with horseradish & lemon juice to taste. ♥

SAUSAGE IN★BRIOCHE

375° Makes 25 slices

This is so delicious & not a bit difficult.♥

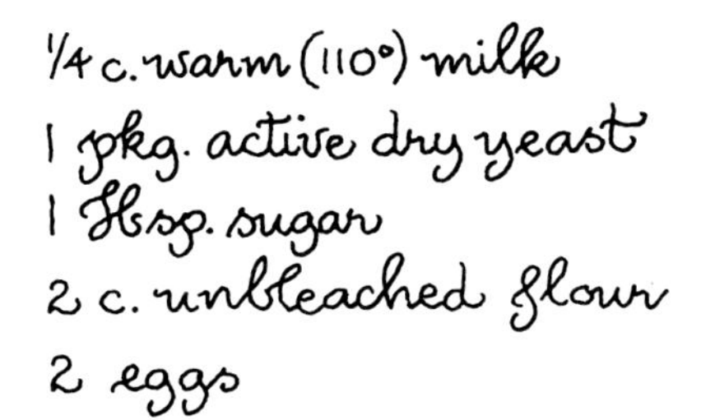

- 1/4 c. warm (110°) milk
- 1 pkg. active dry yeast
- 1 Tbsp. sugar
- 2 c. unbleached flour
- 2 eggs
- 1/2 c. butter, softened
- 3 Tbsp. butter, melted
- 1 lb. ring fully cooked Polish Kielbasa, cut in half
- 1 egg white + 1 tsp. water

This can be made 1 day ahead. Put warm milk in a large bowl, sprinkle in yeast & let stand 5 min., till dissolved. With electric mixer, add sugar & 1/2 c. flour; beat until elastic, about 3 min. Beat in eggs, 1 at a time & gradually beat in rest of flour. Beat in softened butter, 1 Tbsp. at a time. Put the dough in a large buttered bowl, brush on melted butter, cover bowl with dish towel & let rise in a warm place until doubled (about 1½ hrs.). Punch or stir dough down (let the air out) & divide in half. On a floured board, press one half of dough into a 4" x 12" rectangle. Place a sausage half length-wise on dough & gently fold dough over sausage, pinching closed — make sure sausage is totally enclosed. Place seam side down on greased baking sheet. Repeat with remaining dough & sausage.

You may cover & refrigerate up to 1 day — OR, preheat oven to 375° — let loaves rise, again covered in a warm place, till nicely puffed — about 40 min. (If refrigerated overnight, let rise 1¼ hrs.) Brush egg white / water mixture over entire surface of both loaves. Bake 20-25 min., till brown. Serve warm with a serrated knife for slicing & some good mustard.♥ Delicious with soup for a cozy dinner, too! ♥

CAVIAR & OYSTERS

This is a classic for a small, elegant, before-the-fire Christmas get-together for very good friends. It is a wonderful beginning for an evening at the theatre, or before the big Christmas dance. Fill the room with candlelight & roses.

Menu

Fresh, raw oysters on the half shell, served on a trayful of chipped ice with sliced lemon wedges.

The finest caviar, Beluga or Sevruga, served in a non-metal bowl set in ice chips, with a bone or glass spoon. Alongside, serve toasted thin-sliced bread in points, stars, or heart shapes.

Iced bottles of the finest cold "Stars"~

"O, COME QUICKLY, I AM DRINKING STARS!"
SO SAYETH DOM PERIGNON UPON HIS DISCOVERY OF CHAMPAGNE

champagne~served in the most delicate glasses you can find.

Fairy Cones

350° Makes 4 dozen

Something sweet for the buffet table.

Thin, lacy cookies filled with lightly brandied whipped cream ~ a tray of these goes very fast! They are prettiest when filled with a pastry bag & star tip, but you can also do it with a spoon.

- 1/2 c. unsalted butter, cut into bits
- 1/4 c. light corn syrup
- 1/4 c. plus 2 Tbsp. molasses
- 1/4 c. sugar
- 1 c. flour
- 4 tsp. brandy
- 1 tsp. ground ginger
- 1/2 tsp. ground allspice

- 2 c. whipping cream
- 2 Tbsp. brandy
- 1/4 c. powdered sugar, sifted

Preheat oven to 350°. Heat butter, corn syrup, molasses & sugar in top of double boiler over simmering water. Stir constantly till sugar is dissolved. Remove from heat, but leave over hot water. Stir in flour, brandy & spices till smooth. Butter cookie sheets & drop rounded teaspoons of batter, spacing 4" apart. Bake approx. 6 min., till spread & golden. Remove from oven, cool 30 seconds. Working quickly, lift off pan & gently form into cone shape. If cookie becomes too stiff to work, return to oven briefly & it will soften again. Repeat with remaining batter till all are finished, working right along as dough works best when fresh & hot. Store cones in airtight container till ready to fill. Whip cream till soft peaks form, add brandy & sugar; whip cream till firm. Fill pastry bag fitted with star tip & chill. One hour before serving fill cones with brandied cream. After 3-4 hours the filled cookies will lose crispness, so plan accordingly.

BRIE IN PUFF PASTRY

Easy, beautiful & delicious. ♥ 425°

A 2 lb. wheel of Brie cheese, white skin intact
A 17¼ oz. (or so) pkg. frozen puff pastry
1 egg beaten with 1 tsp. water

Thaw pastry till manageable. Cut one sheet into a 10" circle. Place it on parchment paper on a baking sheet. Roll out second sheet of pastry till large enough to cut an 11" circle. Brush water around edge of lower circle. Place larger circle over Brie; press edges of circles together. Using a sharp knife, scallop around edge. (Roll out pastry scraps to ⅛" thick & refrigerate.) To make a chimney for steam to escape: wrap a 1" × 1½" strip of aluminum foil around a pencil. Cut a ¼" hole into center of top, but don't cut the cheese — insert the chimney. From rolled out pastry scraps, cut out little holly leaves & berries, or Christmas trees, or hearts, or whatever you like — brush one side with water & arrange on top of wheel. Refrigerate till 45 min. before serving. Place in freezer for 20 min. Preheat oven to 425° — brush pastry with egg wash. Bake for 25 min. till puffy & golden brown. Serve with hot French bread, crackers, & red & green seedless grapes. ♥

STAR CROUTONS

Float them in soups, toss them in salads, give a jarful as a hostess gift— these starry shapes add a Christmas touch to everything.

1 tiny star-shaped cutter — 1"
a good dense white bread
2 parts butter to:
1 part olive oil
2 or 3 minced garlic cloves, even better put through garlic press

Cut out lots of star shapes from bread. In a large skillet melt butter with oil — add the garlic. Toss the cut-out bread in the butter & oil — the star points are fragile, so be gentle. Don't over-crowd the pan. Toast on both sides. Cool completely & store in airtight container.

Heart shapes, too, are sweet for a romantic evening.

COCONUT SHRIMP

Makes about 40 pieces

Big crunchy bites—everybody loves them ♥. I'll answer your questions: yes, do use medium shrimp & do cut them in half. No, the coconut doesn't make them too sweet. And yes, you can make them ahead ♥.

1 lb. med. shrimp, peeled & deveined
1 egg
3/4 c. pineapple juice
1 1/4 c. flour
vegetable oil for frying
2 7-oz pkgs. shredded coconut
For dipping: Dijon mustard, or catsup mixed with horseradish, or wasabi thinned with soy sauce to taste, with a side dish of pickled ginger.

Cut shrimp in half lengthwise & set aside. Combine egg & pineapple juice; gradually stir in flour, beating till smooth. Pour 1½" vegetable oil into a large skillet—heat to med. high, about 375°. Put the coconut in a shallow bowl. Dip shrimp in batter, then coat with coconut. Fry a few at a time, about 4 min. till golden, both sides. Drain on paper towels. Serve hot with one of the sauces above (my favorite is the one with wasabi). You can fry them ahead, refrigerate 1 day & reheat in a preheated 350° oven for about 5 min. ♥

Tip: When you're having a large cocktail party—don't bring out all the food at once—hold back something special so you can add a little excitement to the party later. ♥

Welcome them home for Christmas with these sandwich plates.

SMOKED SALMON PLATTER

1 smoked salmon, the nicest you can find
cream cheese, softened
pumpernickel cocktail bread
minced red onion
capers
fresh parsley sprigs & lemon wedges

Lay the whole smoked salmon in the center of a large platter or tray. Spread cream cheese on cocktail bread; lightly sprinkle minced onion over each slice. Overlap cream cheese slices around salmon, sprinkle capers over all & garnish with parsley & lemon wedges. Delicious with a crisp cold glass of white wine.

HEART-SHAPED CUCUMBER SANDWICHES

good quality, firm white bread
mayonnaise
cucumbers, peeled & very thinly sliced
freshly ground pepper (no salt)

Cut bread into hearts with a 3" heart-shaped cookie cutter. Thinly spread one heart shape with mayonnaise. Arrange 2 or 3 slices of cucumber on top; grind over fresh pepper. Cover with another slice of bread. Arrange on a plate & chill. Very nice served with a pot of freshly brewed English tea, or steaming mugs of apple cider.

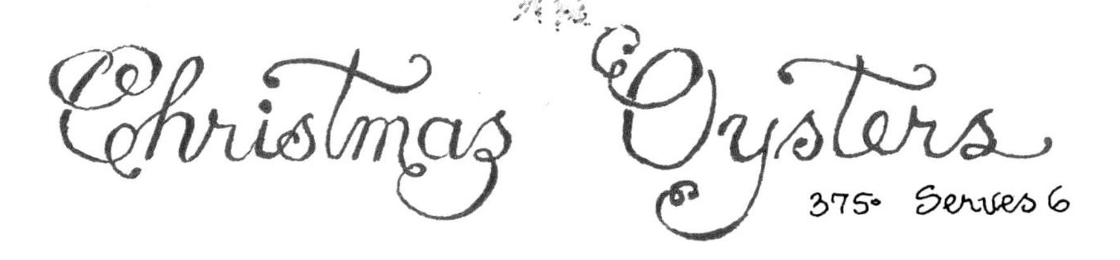

Christmas Oysters

375° Serves 6

The perfect beginning to a special dinner — make them ahead & serve them in front of a fire with a glass of champagne or sherry. Even people who aren't sure about oysters love these. ♥

- 24 of the tiniest oysters you can find
- 1 stick butter
- 1 lg. clove garlic, finely minced
- 2 Tbsp. minced shallots
- 2 Tbsp. fresh lemon juice
- salt & pepper
- 3/4 c. fresh breadcrumbs
- 4 Tbsp. parsley, minced
- opt: 4 slices bacon, fried crisp

Open oysters (your fish person could do this) — leave them on the half shell & put them on a baking sheet. In a skillet melt butter, sauté garlic & shallots 1 min. Stir in lemon juice, salt & pepper. In a small bowl mix together breadcrumbs & parsley; spread over oysters. Drizzle butter over oysters (1 Tbsp. per) — add a little piece of cooked bacon if you like. Cover & refrigerate. When ready, bake at 375° for 20 min. — run under broiler to brown crumbs. Serve. ♥

"The world is my country,
all mankind are my brethren,
and to do good is my religion."

♥ Thomas Paine

Chicken Pâté

Makes 1¼ cups

Serve this creamy spiced pâté with slices of crisp apple & some good crackers. It must be served at room temperature, otherwise it will be crumbly. ♥

½ lb. chicken livers, rinsed
½ c. unsalted butter, softened
2 Tbsp. minced onion
1 Tbsp. minced parsley
1½ tsp. dry mustard
½ tsp. salt
½ tsp. freshly ground nutmeg
⅛ tsp. ground cloves
⅛ tsp. cayenne pepper
2 Tbsp. brandy

In a small saucepan cover livers with water, bring them to a boil; reduce heat & simmer 20 min. Meanwhile, prepare all other ingredients so you can work quickly. Drain livers & purée in food processor. Add all other ingredients except brandy ~ process 1 min. Add brandy in a slow stream & process 10 more seconds. Pour into serving dish, cover & refrigerate. Bring to room temp. before serving. ♥

Chicken Jimmies

375° About 80 pieces

Make these ahead when you're expecting a crowd. ♥

12 boned & skinned chicken thighs
2 c. dry, seasoned bread crumbs
1/2 c. grated Parmesan cheese
1 tsp. salt
1 tsp. onion powder
1/4 tsp. cayenne pepper
2 sticks melted butter

Preheat oven to 375° if you plan to cook them right away. Cut chicken into 1" cubes. Mix together bread crumbs, Parmesan cheese, salt, onion powder & cayenne. Dip chicken in melted butter; roll in bread crumb mixture & place on ungreased cookie sheets (1 layer). Refrigerate till ready to cook. Bake 15-20 min., turning once. Serve ♥

Doggie Treats

350° Makes about 10 ~ 6" bones

This is an appetizer for your dog. It has been, of course, dog-tested & with *wildly* successful results ~ they step on each other to get at these! You can cut them with a bone-shaped cutter ~ but to be honest, the dogs don't seem to care what they're shaped like. ♥ Good gift for favorite pet lovers. ♥

2½ c. whole wheat flour
½ c. powdered dry milk
½ tsp. salt
1 tsp. garlic powder
½ tsp. onion powder
2 tsp. brown sugar
1 tsp. granulated beef bouillon
6 Tbsp. meat drippings (from any meat you have cooked, bacon, etc.)
1 egg, beaten
½ c. ice water

Preheat oven to 350°. Combine first 7 ingredients. Cut in drippings until mixture resembles cornmeal. Mix in egg. Add just enough ice water to make mixture form a ball. Pat dough to ½" thick & cut into desired shapes (little stars are nice for doggie "bites"). Place on a lightly greased cookie sheet & bake 25~30 min. Cool before "serving." ♥

"The gingham dog went 'Bow-wow-wow!'
And the calico cat replied 'Mee-ow!'
The air was littered, an hour or so,
With bits of gingham and calico."
♥ Eugene Field

Decking the Halls

Christmas is a magical time ~ think "magic" as you decorate your home. Shine up all your glass & silver to reflect the light ~ use shiny glass & sparkling things on the tree. Clean windows, mirrors, glass on pictures. Use crystal bowls to hold fruit & candy; glass candle holders, & elegant champagne glasses that ring like clear bells.

Use lots of candles – fat, thin, short & tall ~ everywhere. Set white votives in a bowl of coarse salt for "candles in the snow." Hollow out apples & put in candles. For parties & Christmas Eve, light the house mostly with candles, Christmas tree lights, & a fire in the fireplace — magic!

Sugared fruit: a very elegant & old-fashioned decoration or centerpiece ~ the fruit looks frosted & icy. Dip plums, red grapes, peaches, apples, etc. into egg white & roll in sugar. Put in a pretty bowl.

Drape garlands of pine over mantles, around mirrors, up stairs. Use boughs of holly, rosemary sprigs, English Ivy, poinsettias, mistletoe, paperwhites, pine wreaths, & clumps of baby's breath to decorate. Christmas trees in the kitchen, guest room, children's room.

Bowls of pinecones, apples, pomegranates, cranberries, holly, cinnamon bundles, whole nuts in their shells, tangerines & oranges studded with cloves. Simmer cloves, citrus peel, ginger, cinnamon & nutmeg for good smells.

Flowers: red & pink roses, white lilac, baby's breath, white tulips ~ something low, simple & elegant for the Christmas table.

Tape your Christmas cards around a doorway, window, or mirror.

HO
HO
HO

Decking the Halls

Luminarias are usually made by putting sand in the bottom of a brown paper bag, then setting a votive candle in the sand. When lit, they make wonderful path lighters or front porch decorations. This year, at the last minute, I wanted one to greet guests on the porch, but I had no sand & no brown paper bag. I found a beautiful bag with the face of an angel on it & set the candle in grass seed! The light shone through & the angel face was beautiful. Later it came inside to decorate the hearth. ♥

A pumpkin cut with stars all over & lit with a candle is another fun porch light. Tie a wreath to the bumper of your car.

Fa-la-la

Play Christmas music ~ classical & "the boys" Frank, Bing, Dean & Nat.

Hang pictures of friends & family from previous Christmases on your refrigerator with little magnets. Set out the photo album to encourage remembrance. Set up framed pictures of family, especially those unable to be present. ♥

Candy houses, cinnamon hearts, chocolate kisses, plates of cookies, candy canes, ribbon candy, gingerbread houses, loaves of bread, popcorn balls & candied apples all perk things up. Use children's toys to decorate: blocks, trains & teddy bears.

For the table: a colorful quilt, a special lace tablecloth, or even a nice white bedspread. Hang stockings (with care) at fireplace or on backs of chairs.

Tie ribbon around the dog's neck, put a bell on the cat, dress up your children, put on a cute apron, send your mom a corsage, get dad a boutonniere, put jingle bells on the baby's shoes. Fill your house with love. ♥

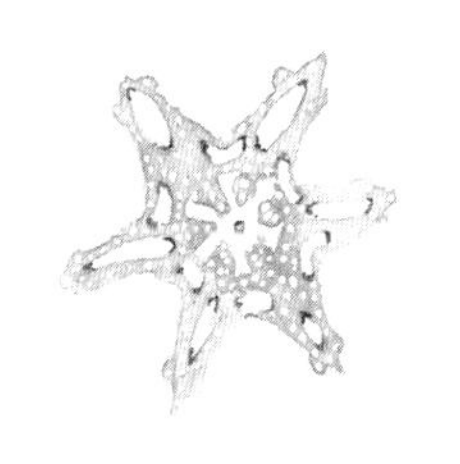

"But in this season it is well to reassert that the hope of mankind rests in faith. As man thinketh, so he is. Nothing much happens unless you believe in it, and believing there is hope for the world is a way to move toward it."

Gladys Taber

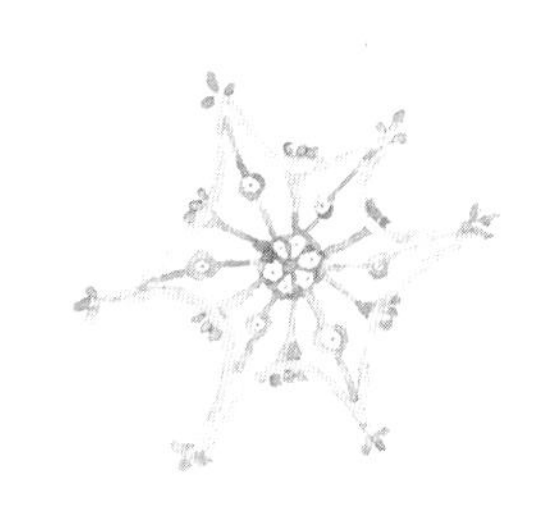

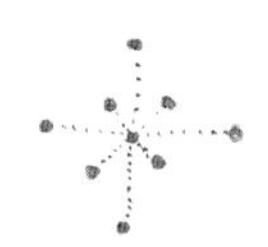

NOGS & GROGS
PUNCH & TEA

"Animal crackers, and cocoa to drink,
That is the finest of suppers, I think;
When I'm grown up and can have what I please
I think I shall always insist upon these."
♡ Christopher Morley

LITTLE LIBATIONS

Hot Buttered Rum: Keep this on hand for "pop-in" guests. Cream 1 lb. softened butter with 2 lbs. brown sugar. Stir in 1 tsp. vanilla, 1 Tbsp. cinnamon, & 1/2 tsp. nutmeg. (Keep refrigerated) To serve: put 1 Tbsp. of butter mix in a mug; add 1 oz. dark rum & 6 oz. boiling water. Stir & serve. ♡

Chocolate Mint: Pour your hot chocolate over a peppermint tea bag & allow it to steep to taste. If you'd like a bit more of a zing to your cocoa, add an oz. of Peppermint Schnapps. ♡

Mint Julep: My girlfriend Margot starts her famous Mint Juleps in the summertime. Fresh mint is not easy to get in December on this little island ~ so in August she pours out about 1/4c. from a fifth of Jack Daniel's (bourbon whiskey). In its place she puts a cup of crushed & twisted fresh mint leaves. It steeps until Christmas when she serves it with a bit of sugar in a silver cup with lots of shaved ice. Straws are de rigueur (glass ones are best); if you can find it, fresh mint for garnish is wonderful. ♡

Angel Tea: This isn't tea at all & nobody seems to know why we call it that! It's actually a dry, sparkly, light wine punch ~ good if you're looking to get away from the usual cream punches & nogs. Combine 2 bottles very good dry white wine with 1 bottle of plain seltzer water & 3 Tbsp. Angostura bitters. Garnish with thin slices of lemon & lime, if you like & serve from pitchers over ice. ♡

ICED VODKA WITH SWEETHEART ROSES

This is so beautiful at a party ~ & it only gets prettier as the ice melts and the rose petals begin to stick through. Make a private little caviar party even more romantic with this. ♥

- 1 bottle good Russian vodka
- 1 clean, empty, narrow bottle with a long neck, and a top
- 1 clean, empty, ½ gallon milk carton, with the top cut off, or just opened up
- 6 ~ 8 sweetheart roses
- extra greenery, like box or rosemary, if you like

I have an old olive oil bottle I use for this ~ it is narrow, so it fits into the milk carton with space left over for the roses & a good thick wall of ice. It also has a long neck to stick out the top, & a cork. Funnel the vodka into the bottle, cork it, and set the bottle into milk carton. Fill to neck with water & surround with roses & greenery ~ arranging as best you can, unfolding leaves; everything totally under water. Freeze it (vodka doesn't freeze). When it's time to serve, peel off milk carton, & set into rimmed bowl with more greenery. Gorgeous, eh? ♥

SPICED CIDER

MAKES 9 CUPS

A nice "welcome home" on a cold evening. ♥

- 2 qts. apple cider
- 3 cinnamon sticks
- 40 whole cloves
- 1 tsp. nutmeg
- 2 c. fresh orange juice
- 1/2 c. fresh lemon juice
- 2 strips orange peel
- rum, opt.

Boil cider, cinnamon, cloves, nutmeg together for 15 min. Add juices & orange peel (try not to get white pith with peel). Serve hot ~ with rum if you like. ♥

CHOCOLATE MINT COFFEE

The perfect way to end an evening.♥
Serves 4

½ c. whipping cream
2 Tbsp. powdered sugar
1 tsp. vanilla
1 oz. German sweet chocolate—grated
2 c. strong hot coffee
8 Tbsp. peppermint schnapps
chocolate curls

Beat cream with sugar & vanilla until soft peaks form. Fold in grated chocolate. Pour hot coffee evenly into 4 mugs & add 2 Tbsp. schnapps to each. Spoon on whipped cream. Garnish with chocolate curls & serve immediately. ♥

Classic Egg Nog

Makes 1 gal. + 2~4 c.

Not the sticky-sweet stuff in the markets — this very traditional egg nog has an elegant, sophisticated flavor & should be served in a special bowl. ♥

12 eggs, separated
1 c. sugar
1½ c. good bourbon
½ c. good brandy
1 c. heavy cream
3 c. whole milk
3 c. half & half
1¼ tsp. freshly ground nutmeg

In a lg. bowl, beat egg yolks & sugar on low speed with electric mixer till blended. Turn mixer to high & beat till thick & pale colored — about 10 min. Add bourbon & brandy in a thin drizzle while continuing to beat at high speed. Cover & refrigerate at least 20 min. Separately, whip egg whites & cream to firm peaks. Pour chilled egg yolk mixture into a lg. punch bowl; add milk, half & half, & nutmeg. Gently fold in egg whites & cream — till just blended. Sprinkle with a bit more nutmeg & serve. ♥

Peach Cream

Delicious for Christmas Brunch ~ tastes like a Creamsicle. ♥

1 oz. peach schnapps
1 oz. fresh orange juice
2 oz. vanilla ice cream
1/2 c. crushed ice

For each drink, put all of the above in a blender & blend 30 seconds. Serve. ♥

Makes 1 drink

Whip the cream & set up each mug to the point of adding coffee, & serving this delicious spiced drink will be easy♥.

1 oz. dark rum
2 whole cloves
1 tsp. sugar
1 strip orange rind ½" x 4"
8 oz. strong hot coffee
whipped cream
freshly grated nutmeg

Place rum, cloves, & sugar in a lg. mug. Twist the orange rind to release the oils & add it to the mug. Pour in hot coffee, top with whipped cream & sprinkle with nutmeg. Serve♥.

SOBER WATER

This delicious drink (which is even safe for the designated drivers in the group) is pretty to look at & festive to taste: over ice, fill a glass with sparkling water & top with a couple of shakes of Angostura bitters, to taste. ♥

Make a wish with

ELFIN WINE

Serves 6~8

This is the celebratory drink supposedly made by the elves of the Alps many, many years ago. The delicious wine-soaked, good-luck walnuts you find in the bottom of your cup take the place of the magical gold nuggets of yore, which I'm sure were nice, but a little tough on the tummy! ♥

2 bottles of good red wine (Beaujolais)
3 almond tea bags
6 whole allspice
3 cinnamon sticks
8 whole cloves
2 tsp. vanilla
walnut halves

Combine 1st 6 ingredients in a large saucepan & slowly bring to a simmer; simmer 5 min. Drop 2 walnut halves in the bottom of each cup. Strain the wine as you fill the cups. Make a wish on each walnut half when you reach the bottom of your cup. ♥

Sandra Boynton

Snow Angels

PLOP **DOWN** IN THE SNOW ON YOUR **BACK** ~ **WA**VE YOUR ARMS AND LEGS ~ GET UP AND THERE WILL BE AN ANGEL IMPRINT IN THE SNOW. DO THE WHOLE YARD! ♥

Soap Snow

NO SNOW? "PAINT" TIPS OF TREE BRANCHES WITH THIS. IT WILL HARDEN.
2 C. IVORY SNOW & 1/2 C. WATER ~ BEAT W/ ELECTRIC MIXER ♥.

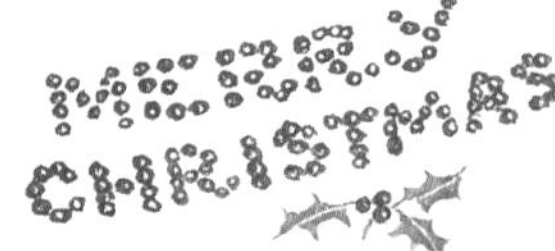

TAKE A PICTURE OF YOUR HOUSE IN THE SNOW, OR WRITE A MESSAGE IN THE SNOW WITH CRANBERRIES OR HOLLY BERRIES ~ TAKE A PICTURE OF IT ~ MAKE LOTS OF COPIES AND SEND THEM OUT AS CHRISTMAS POSTCARDS ♥.

MAKE SNOW PEOPLE: USE OLD HATS, SCARVES, GLOVES; PUT A FAT CANDLE IN HANDS. MAKE SCULPTURES: SWANS & DUCKS; YOU CAN USE FOOD COLORING FOR THEIR BILLS. SNOW CASTLES: USE BUCKETS, FUNNELS, & BOXES FOR MOLDS; TWIGS & ICICLES TO DECORATE. ♥

Snow Sweets

SNOW CONES: POUR FRUIT JUICES OVER FRESH-FALLEN SNOW: ORANGE, CRANBERRY, OR PINEAPPLE JUICE.
SUGAR ON SNOW: HEAT REAL MAPLE SYRUP TO 250°; DON'T STIR. POUR OVER A BOWL OF CLEAN SNOW. ♥

"The cold wind burns my face,
and blows
It's frosty pepper up my nose."

Robt. Louis Stevenson

THE MAGIC OF SNOW

On December 23rd I had to go downtown to do a bit more shopping. We hadn't had any snow yet, but we were in the perfect place for Christmas ~ our Main Street is only 3 blocks long & the charming New England stores were decorated with tiny white lights, Christmas wreaths & Santa faces. I came out of the store with my packages just as it started to snow. It came down so soft & light; so quietly, landing on my shoulders, in my hair, on my nose. I was humming Christmas carols — everyone had smiles on their faces & Christmas had really begun.

When the snow comes, everything changes ~ you see special things. A horse-drawn wagon filled with happy people jingle-jangles down my street. My holly trees are heavy with snow, but the spiky green leaves & red berries still show through. There are hillsides of brightly dressed children playing with their sleds — skaters are on the ponds, their colorful scarves streaming out behind them. When I go for a walk my boots make a wonderful crunch, the chill air burns my face & I come back, refreshed, to a crackling fire & a cozy house. Time to cook something.

At night the sky is black & the stars glitter & you can smell the smoke from someone's chimney. There are flocks of wild geese, black & brown against the snow; they take off in honking unison ~ you can hear their wings beating the air. I love the fat bundles of winter children, their rosy red cheeks peeking out of their funny knitted caps. There's a gnarled old tree in Edgartown where they've hung loads of wax pears & on a lower branch is a brightly painted partridge.

My point is, if you don't live in snow country, try to take a Christmas vacation ~ get yourself a cozy house nestled in the snow ~ do winter things. Forget about presents ~ this will be the best gift of all

"Children need Christmas trees, and not artificial ones either. The artificial ones have no fragrance, and some of them play tunes, which is dreadful to think of."

♥ Gladys Taber

CHRISTMAS IS FOR CHILDREN

On the first day of Christmas vacation, let your child choose the dinner menu. Make this a Xmas tradition. ♥

Make a "Yay! Christmas Vacation!" banner to hang over the front door to welcome them home. ♥

Start a hope chest for boys and girls. Put in Great G'ma's hand embroidered dish towels, Aunt Mary's famous sugar cookie recipe; add a sterling silver place setting each year and a special bottle of wine to drink on their wedding day. Put in their baby books, keepsakes, photos and mementos. Have fun! ♥

On Christmas Eve I used to run around outside with jingle bells at the windows ~ the little kids went wild with excitement! ♥

CELEBRATE THE WONDER

Fill your child's closet with balloons ~ write messages on them ~ watch his eyes light up.

Have a special Christmas party just for children. A vinyl tablecloth is nice ~ use tiny teddy bears (for them to keep) to hold placecards. Make decorations, take flowers to a convalescent home & sing some carols, eat cake & cookies, make a candy house (there are kits now), read a Christmas story & play pin the star to the tree. Scavenger hunts are great for older children. ♥

Love Note: Mom and Dad make a "Joey sandwich" ~ they hug each other & put Joey in the middle. ♥

Listen to your children: sometimes they'll be wanting to show their love when you are busy ~ try to stop and return their love with special hugs and kisses. ♥

When you take them Christmas shopping, include something fun just for them. Take time to visit Santa, sit down for a chocolate eclair, look at displays, or shop for Daddy. ♥

SWEET NOTHINGS

Bundle up your children and take them to midnight services (even if you have to wake them). It can be magical and awe inspiring. ♥

Give something to charity every year and discuss it all with your children. Encourage them to become citizens of the world. ♥

Let your children snuggle into bed with you on a snowy Christmas morning. ♥

Make a photo album especially for your child for a Christmas present. Star him, his friends, his pets, him on vacation ~ include cartoons, quotes, newspaper headlines, and a big "I love you." ♥

A surprise bouquet of flowers will let your child know how special she is ♥. (Or he is.)

Read them a Christmas story, one chapter each night ~ to end the day in a relaxing family atmosphere. ♥

Children are the hope for the future, shower them with love. ♥

CHRISTMAS MEMORIES

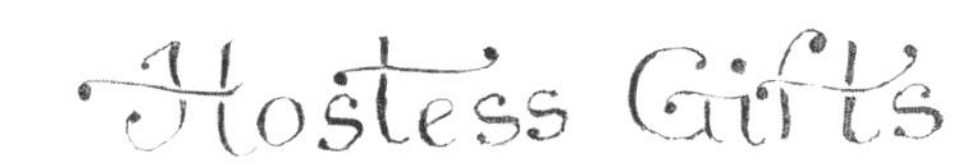

If you are going to spend a holiday weekend with family or friends, or simply going to dinner, a thoughtful gift will be a nice surprise for your host or hostess. ♥ Something personal or something for the house — extravagant, simple, or funny & always with love. ♥

MAKE A PIN FROM AN ANTIQUE STERLING SALT SPOON FOR YOUR COOK FRIENDS. ♥

A FAVORITE COOKBOOK, GARDEN, OR TRAVEL BOOK.

A BERIBBONED JAR OF STAR CROUTONS. ☆ (P. 15)

A NICE HUNK OF REGGIANO CHEESE WITH A HAND GRATER. ♥

A GOOD PEPPERMILL AND A JAR OF FINE PEPPERCORNS. ♥

STRIPED SOCKS. ♥

VODKA AND SWEETHEART ROSES. ♥ (P. 27)

CHRISTMAS TIE

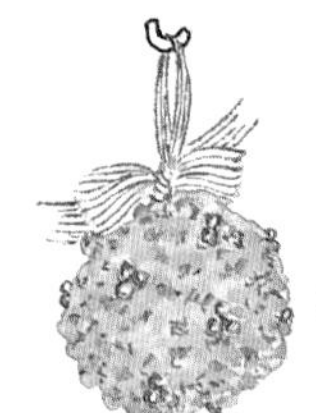

A KISSING BALL XXX

HAVE A MUSICIAN ARRIVE FOR A SURPRISE SERENADE. ♥

A FLOWERED TEACUP, TEA BALL, AND A CAN OF LOOSE ENGLISH TEA. ♥

MOST PEOPLE COLLECT SOMETHING ~ ADD TO THEIR COLLECTION OR USE THE IDEAS ON PAGE 104 TO HELP THEM START ONE. ♥

A GLASS DOME ON A FLOWERED CHINA PLATE, LINED WITH A DOILY ~ FILLED WITH COOKIES OR SCONES. ♥

Side Dishes

Vegetables
Stuffings
Salads

"Then I would be slap-dashing home, the gravy smell of the dinners of others, the bird smell, the brandy, the pudding and mince, coiling up to my nostrils..." ♥ Dylan Thomas

MINTY PEAS

Serves 10

⅓ c. water
3 Tbsp. butter
1 Tbsp. dried peppermint leaves
3 10-oz. pkgs. frozen baby peas

Place water, butter, & mint in a large saucepan & bring to a boil ~ let boil 1 min. Add frozen peas, cover & cook 3 min. Toss gently & serve. ♥

WILD RICE & APPLES

325° Makes 8 cups

You can stuff this into chickens, turkeys, or game hens, but mostly I just bake it in the oven – the fruit & nuts are a good complement to fish or fowl. It can be made ahead & is great for a big buffet. ♥

- ½ lb. wild rice, cooked
- ½ c. butter, melted
- ½ lb. mushrooms, sliced
- 2 Tbsp. minced onion
- 1 lg. tart apple, peeled, cored, & chopped
- 1 c. fresh bread crumbs
- ½ c. walnuts, chopped
- ¼ c. candied orange peel (homemade p. 91), finely chopped
- ¼ c. fresh orange juice

To cook the rice: add rice to 4 c. boiling water & 1 tsp. salt. Return to boil, stir, reduce to simmer, cover & cook 50 min. Uncover, fluff with fork & continue to simmer 5 more min. Drain any excess liquid. Preheat oven to 325°. Melt butter & use 3 Tbsp. of it to lightly sauté mushroom & onions. Add this mixture to cooked rice, & put in all other ingredients, including the remaining melted butter. Mix well & put into a 2 qt. casserole. Cover & bake 35 min. (It may be refrigerated, covered, until ready to bake; or if you use it as a stuffing, don't bake, just stuff & cook it inside the bird.) ♥

"...how truly is a kind heart a fountain of gladness, making everything in its vicinity to freshen into smiles!" ♥ Washington Irving

ROASTED SHALLOTS

350° Serves 4

Delicious when served with some of the sweet & fruited vegetables & sauces we love at Christmas ♥

20 to 24 shallots
2 Tbsp. olive oil
fresh cracked pepper

Preheat oven to 350°. Remove outer skins & roots of shallots. Place the shallots in one layer in a baking pan & pour oil over ; toss to coat. Grind fresh pepper over & roast 15 min. Turn them all over & roast 15 min. more. Serve. ♥

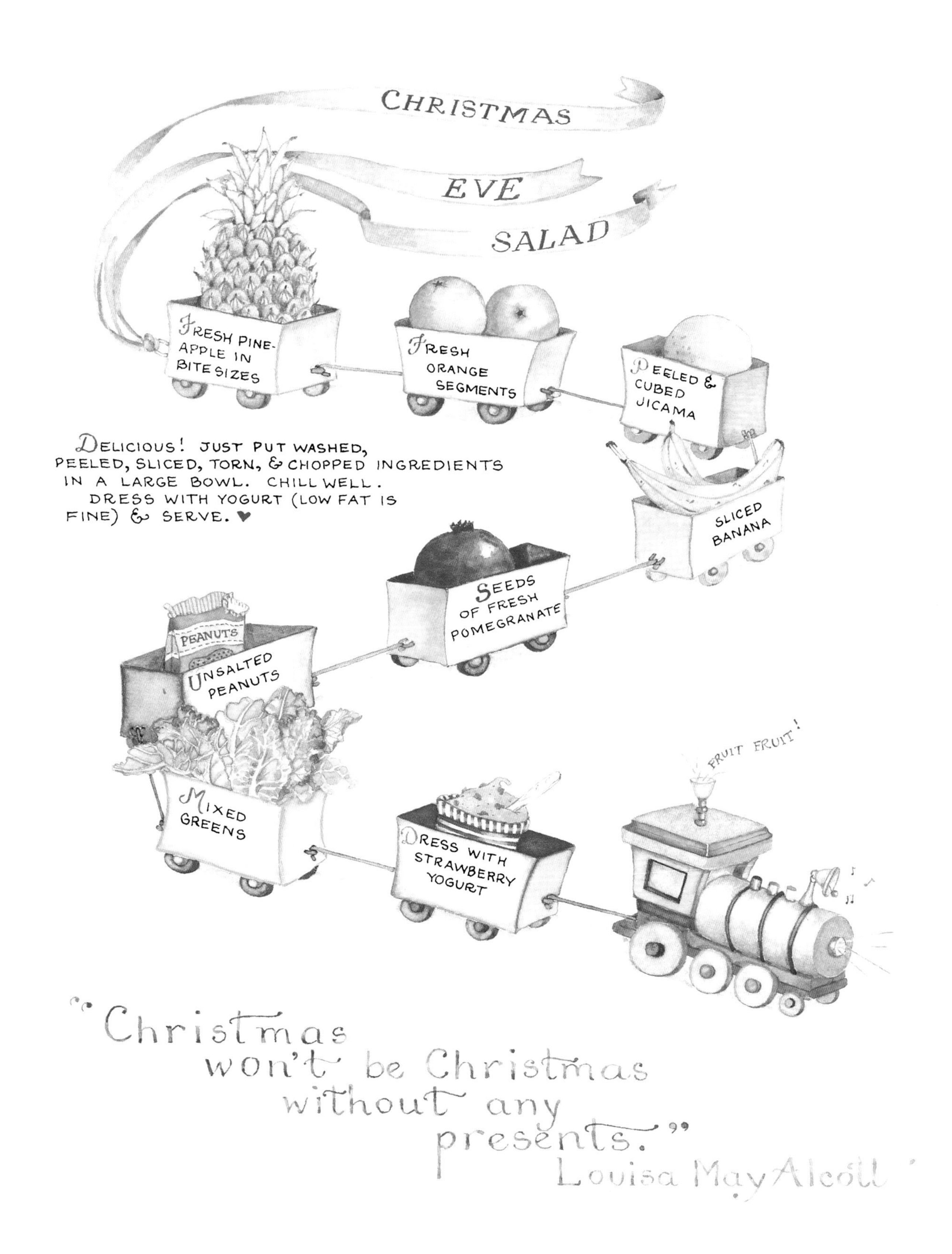
CHRISTMAS
EVE
SALAD
FRESH PINE-APPLE IN BITE SIZES
FRESH ORANGE SEGMENTS
PEELED & CUBED JICAMA
SLICED BANANA
SEEDS OF FRESH POMEGRANATE
PEANUTS
UNSALTED PEANUTS
MIXED GREENS
DRESS WITH STRAWBERRY YOGURT
FRUIT FRUIT!
DELICIOUS! JUST PUT WASHED, PEELED, SLICED, TORN, & CHOPPED INGREDIENTS IN A LARGE BOWL. CHILL WELL.
DRESS WITH YOGURT (LOW FAT IS FINE) & SERVE. ♥
"Christmas won't be Christmas without any presents."
Louisa May Alcott

VEGETABLE SAUTÉ WITH ROASTED GARLIC

275° Serves 4

Colorful & delicious — most of this dish can be made ahead.

- 24 small, unpeeled garlic cloves
- 1 Tbsp. olive oil
- 3/4 lbs. broccoli, in bite-sized pieces
- 3/4 lbs. baby carrots, peeled & trimmed
- 1 Tbsp. sugar
- 3 Tbsp. unsalted (sweet) butter
- 2 Tbsp. brandy
- 2 Tbsp. chopped parsley
- salt & pepper, to taste

Preheat oven to 275°. Add garlic to 2 c. boiling water — boil 3 min., drain. Peel & trim root ends. Heat oil in a small oven-proof skillet — add garlic cloves & toss. Cover loosely with foil, bake 1/2 hr., stirring once. Remove foil, bake 10 min. more, till tender. Remove from oven & set aside. Boil broccoli in 3 c. water with 1/2 tsp. salt for 3 min., drain & set aside. Add sugar & carrots to 3 c. boiling water with 1/2 tsp. salt. Boil till just tender (about 10 min.). Drain & set aside. When ready to serve, melt butter in a lg. heavy skillet. Add vegetables to pan, heat through, tossing gently. Warm the brandy, light it & pour over vegetables — shake pan till flame expires. Sprinkle with parsley & salt & pepper. Serve.

Ginger Squash

Serves 8

4 med. butternut squash
1 Tbsp. peeled & minced fresh ginger
2 Tbsp. honey
3 Tbsp. sweet butter
½ tsp. freshly ground pepper

Halve squash lengthwise – discard seeds & strings. Using a melon baller, scoop balls from the squash – or, if you'd rather, you can cube it. Add the squash to 3 qts. of boiling water (with 1 Tbsp. salt) & cook 5 min., till tender. (You may have to do this in 2 batches – use a slotted spoon to remove first batch to colander.) Meantime, in a small saucepan, heat ginger, honey & butter, stirring till melted, blended & hot. Put the squash in a serving dish, pour ginger butter over, sprinkle with pepper & serve. ♥

"To all, to each, a fair good night,
And pleasing dreams; and
slumbers light." ♥ Sir Walter Scott

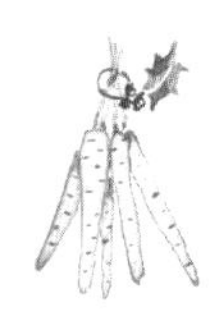

CARROTS IN ORANGE-GINGER SAUCE

Serves 6~8

12 med. carrots
juice of 4 oranges
2 tsp. grated orange rind
2 tsp. grated fresh ginger
2 tsp. flour
½ tsp. salt
4 Tbsp. butter

Peel carrots & cut them into thin strips 2½"~3" long. Boil them till barely tender — remove from heat but do not drain (they'll continue cooking & stay hot while you make the sauce). In another pan whisk together remaining ingredients, except butter, over med. heat until thickened. Add butter & cook till melted. Drain carrots, pour sauce over & stir to coat. You can keep them in a warm oven till ready to serve. ♡

"Not believe in Santa Claus! You might as well not believe in fairies!"
♥ Frank Church

ORANGE WATERCRESS SALAD

Serves 8

Refreshing pieces of juicy orange bits are a delicious "find" in a heavy holiday meal.

- 1 head Belgian endive – coarsely chopped
- 3 bunches watercress, washed, tough stems removed
- 2 oranges, peeled, seeded & sectioned – cut the sections in half
- 1 orange rind, grated (no white pith)
- 1/3 c. olive oil
- 3 Tbsp. white wine vinegar
- 1 tsp. Dijon mustard
- 1 tsp. minced parsley
- 1 Tbsp. grated Parmesan
- salt & freshly ground pepper, to taste

Note: Endive can be very bitter – if this is the case, get another head of watercress & omit endive – or sprinkle over a little bit just for contrast.

Put the greens in your serving bowl with orange pieces – refrigerate till serving time. Put all other ingredients in a shaker jar – shake well to mix. Refrigerate. To serve: shake dressing, pour over salad & toss gently.

"On with the dance!
Let joy be unconfined."
Lord Byron

Creamed Onions

Serves 4

I serve this old & elegant recipe in the same faded, flowered China dish every year, with the same large-bowled silver child's spoon alongside. A traditional dish in a traditional dish ♥.

1 pt. tiniest white onions, peeled & trimmed
2 Tbsp. unsalted butter
½ c. chicken broth
½ c. dry white wine
1 c. heavy cream
pinch o' salt
pinch o' white pepper
⅛ tsp. fresh nutmeg
1 tsp. minced parsley

In a large covered skillet, simmer peeled onions in butter, broth & wine about 20 min., till tender. Add cream & boil, uncovered, 4-5 min. till slightly thickened. Stir in salt, white pepper & nutmeg. Pour into serving dish, & sprinkle with parsley. ♥

Sweet Potato Casserole With Walnuts

350° Serves 8

As far as I'm concerned this is the last word in sweet potatoes ~ just delicious! You can make them ahead if you like. ♥

4 c. sweet potatoes, cooked & mashed
8 oz. cream cheese, softened
½ c. unsalted butter, softened
2 eggs, beaten
¼ c. brown sugar
2½ Tbsp. dry sherry
¼ tsp. salt
¾ c. black walnuts, chopped
½ tsp. nutmeg, freshly grated if possible

Preheat oven to 350°. With electric mixer (not food processor) whip all ingredients, except walnuts & nutmeg, until light. Stir in walnuts & put into a buttered casserole. Spread evenly & grate fresh nutmeg over the top. Bake 45 min. till golden. ♥

"Close by the jolly fire I sit
To warm my frozen bones a bit."
Robt. Louis Stevenson ♥

SLICED ORANGES

Serves 10

Serve a beautiful platter of ice cold oranges with almost anything — pork, lamb, turkey — even with waffles — yum. ♥ A little troublesome to peel — guess that's why they seem so special. ♥

10 navel oranges
grated rind of 1 lime & 1 lemon
juice of 1 lime & 1 lemon
2 Tbsp. sugar

Peel 9 oranges as gently as possible & remove all the white pith — cut it off with a sharp knife. Grate the rinds of lime & lemon into small bowl — again, no white pith. Add the juice of the remaining orange, the lime & the lemon; blend in sugar. Thinly slice oranges & arrange on platter. Pour juice mixture over oranges. Cover & refrigerate — "baste" every so often with accumulated juices. ♥

TASTE TREAT

I just found the biggest, fattest, juiciest, most delectable & gorgeous dried apricots I've ever tasted — they come from Australia in a wooden box & I ordered them from the Williams-Sonoma catalog. Thought you'd like to know! ♥

CREAMED SPINACH

Serves 6

Lightly spiced, with a touch of nutmeg & pieces of bacon for bite ~ a lovely holiday side dish all dressed up with slivered egg whites & riced yolks.

2 lbs. fresh spinach, washed & stemmed
4 slices bacon, crisp fried ~ save fat
1 Tbsp. butter
2 Tbsp. minced onion
1/4 c. unbleached flour
1 c. chicken stock } mixed
1 c. whole milk }
1/4 tsp. freshly ground pepper
freshly ground nutmeg
3 hard-boiled eggs, yolks separated

(Hard boil the eggs.) Put washed spinach in a lg. pot; do not add water. Cover & simmer 15 min., drain & chop fine. Set aside. Cook the bacon & also set aside. Add butter to bacon fat ~ sauté onions in fat 1 min. Stirring constantly, add flour & cook over med. heat 5 min., or until light brown. While stirring, slowly add stock & milk mixture ~ then pepper. Simmer till thickened. Stir in spinach & crumbled bacon. Pour in to serving dish. Garnish with slivered egg whites & "riced" yolks (which you do by gently pushing through a garlic press). Sprinkle with fresh nutmeg & serve. Can be made ahead, rewarmed, & then garnished.

FRESH FRUIT SALAD

"The essential elements... of the romantic spirit are curiosity and the love of beauty."

♥ *Walter Pater* ♥

Warm Spinach Salad

Serves 6

Very Christmasy looking — the pomegranate seeds & toasted walnuts make it very special ♡.

10 oz. fresh spinach leaves, washed, dried, & stemmed
1 ripe avocado, thinly sliced
1 pomegranate, seeds only
1 c. thinly sliced mushrooms
1/2 c. coarsely chopped walnuts
3 slices bacon
1/4 c. brown sugar
1/2 c. cider vinegar
1/3 c. olive oil
freshly cracked black pepper, about 1/2 tsp.

Place torn spinach leaves, avocado slices, pomegranate seeds, & sliced mushrooms into a large bowl & set aside. In a large, dry skillet, toast walnut pieces over high heat for 1-1½ min. shaking & tossing constantly. Sprinkle over salad. In same skillet, fry bacon till crisp & remove from pan. Pour off all but 1 Tbsp. of fat. Over med. heat, blend in sugar, vinegar, oil, & pepper; heat through, stirring occasionally until sugar is dissolved. Crumble bacon over salad, pour hot dressing over, toss & serve. ♡

TURKEY STUFFING

My grandma's recipe (her mom's, too), & the best there is ~ no namby-pamby bread crumbs or mixes here. Moist & chewy ~ you can add sausage or apples, oysters or chestnuts ~ whatever you like, but plain is fine by me. ♡ For some reason "good" bread doesn't work ~ use the cheap, soft kind, "bunny bread." ♡

- 3 giant loaves cheap bread, 2 white; 1 brown
- 1 c. butter
- 3 med. onions, chopped
- 6 stalks celery, chopped
- 1 jar sage leaves, about ½ c.
- 1 Tbsp. salt, or to taste
- freshly ground pepper
- opt: apples, walnuts, sausage, oysters, etc.

(Three days before turkey day, set the bread out to thoroughly dry.) Put about 6" of the hottest water you can stand to touch in your clean sink. Dip each slice of bread into the water & wring it out well; put it in a large bowl, breaking it up a bit as you go ~ it should be chunky, doughy, chewy. Melt butter in a lg. skillet. Very slowly, sauté onions & celery in butter; do not brown butter. Meanwhile, over the sink, rub sage leaves in your palms, breaking up & discarding woody stems carefully. Put the leaves in with the bread. Pour butter mixture over bread & mix well with your hands (careful not to burn yourself). Add the salt, mix well. It should be a little bit salty ~ the turkey will absorb it (but just a little bit). Add pepper & any other ingredients that suit your fancy. Loosely stuff turkey & bake any left over in a separate covered dish. ♡

"Backward, turn backward, O Time in your flight;
Make me a child again just for tonight." ♡

Elizabeth Akers Allen

GRAVY

Some people get nervous about gravy, we don't make it as often as we once did. But it's so easy ~ just remember that the POINT is to simmer all the flavor possible from the bones, giblets, & skin, along with vegetables, herbs & spices & the flavorful meat drippings from the roasting pan. For stronger flavor, just boil down. Remove fat, thicken with flour/water mixture & voilà!

Turkey Gravy: Put 1 Tbsp. olive oil in a lg. saucepan over med. high heat. Chop neck & giblets (no liver) & brown them quickly in oil. Add 1 chopped onion, 1 chopped carrot, 1 chopped celery stalk, 3 parsley sprigs, 1 bay leaf, 8 peppercorns & 1 tsp. thyme. Add 1 qt. water, stir to remove bits stuck to bottom of pan. Simmer, partially covered for 2 hrs. Add 1 c. white wine & 1 Tbsp. brandy ~ bring to boil ~ boil 5 min. Strain & set aside. Turkey must rest ½ hr. after roasting so remove it to platter & place roasting pan with juices over med. high heat ~ when hot, pour in some stock, mix with pan juices & scrape brown bits from pan. Pour all stock & juices into a wide dish & set it in freezer ~ fat will rise to top ~ remove & discard. Reheat stock & taste for strength. In a jar with a lid, shake together ½ c. water & 6 Tbsp. flour. Slowly add just enough flour mixture to thicken to your liking. Taste, add salt & pepper. ♥

Once upon a time, Mr. and Mrs. Claus started to become unhappy and even began to bicker — they were under a lot of stress with always so much to do. So they took dancing lessons

and they lived happily ever after.

SOMETHING SPECIAL

" 'The first thing you must do,' said the fairy, 'is to go back into the sitting-room and find my magic wand. I'm useless without it.' "
H.E. Todd

Throughout the years I have always tried to look for extra-special ways to celebrate with my friends & family — these are a few of my favorites:

For someone who is far away at Christmas time: gather friends and/or family — everybody dress up! Hold up a big sign that says "We love you, Bud" — take a picture & mail it to Bud. ♡

Send a violinist, or other instrument-toting musician, to a friend's party for a surprise serenade. ♡

Turn a child's drawing into Christmas memories; have it inexpensively printed into cards or notepads. The "right" people will consider them high art. ♡

Hold hands during grace. ♡

Ask your Grandma to describe Christmas as it was when she was a child — ask her to tell you about her parents. Tape her memories & save them for your own children. ♡

Bring Christmas cards containing news from afar to the dinner table & read them aloud. ♡

For newlyweds at Christmas — a box of really wonderful ornaments including one with the year of their 1st Christmas as husband & wife. Add to the collection yearly with a dated ornament. ♡

If you can talk someone into it: an at-home Christmas Eve wedding couldn't be more romantic, with the sparkling tree, candlelight, flowers, champagne & men in tuxedos — oooo la la! ♡

STOCKING STUFFERS

ALL KINDS OF LITTLE TOYS: JACKS AND BALL, A YO-YO, TINY TEDDY BEARS, A MAGNIFYING GLASS, CRAYONS, A SNOWSTORM IN A GLASS, A JUMPROPE, GLIDER PLANES, PADDLE BALLS, LITTLE DOLLS, WATERCOLORS AND BRUSHES, PAPER DOLLS, NOISE MAKERS, & STAR STICKERS. ♥

GIFT CERTIFICATES FOR FOOD, FLOWERS, AND FUN~ TICKETS FOR A PLAY, A CONCERT OR THE LOTTERY. ♥

BEAUTIFUL OLIVE OIL, RED ITALIAN TABLE WINE IN A WICKER CONTAINER, ELEPHANT GARLIC, FANCY TEAS, MUSTARD, JAMS & POPCORN. A WHISK, MUG, VEGETABLE PEELER, KITCHEN SCISSORS, TWINE, OR MEASURING SPOONS. ♥ RECIPES! ♥

BASEBALL, TENNIS BALLS, GOLF BALLS, HEAD AND WRISTBANDS, STOP WATCH, TAPE MEASURE, CALORIE COUNTER, BALL CAP, TICKETS FOR A GAME. ♥

THINK OF HOBBIES AND GIVE ACCORDINGLY; GARDENING, SEWING, PUTTERING IN THE BASEMENT, TRAVELING, READING AND SO ON. ♥

BATHROOM STUFF: BUBBLE BATH, SWEET SOAPS AND LOTIONS, PERFUME, NAIL POLISH, HAIR CUTTING SCISSORS, SEASHELLS, DUCK-SHAPED NAIL BRUSH, A SHOWER CAP, AFTER SHAVE LOTION AND A HAND MIRROR. OH! AND HAIR RIBBONS, BOWS AND CLIPS ~ COMBS AND BRUSHES. ♥ (AND LOOFAHS AND SPONGES.) ♥

MITTENS, SOCKS, SCARVES, "DESIGNER" SHOELACES, SLIPPERS, AND A PAIR OF RED SILK BOXER SHORTS! BRACELET AND PINS AND EARRINGS ~ AND A SILVER MONEY CLIP. LEATHER GLOVES, SILK STOCKINGS, AND A NEEDLEPOINT EYE-GLASS HOLDER. ♥

STATIONERY, BOOKPLATES, POSTAGE STAMPS, DIARY, PEN, PERSONAL CALENDAR, & TELEPHONE BOOK ~ GET THINGS MONOGRAMMED! ♥

GOOD SHARP SCISSORS, MAGNETS FOR THE REFRIGERATOR, TINY AMERICAN FLAGS, CHRISTMAS ORNAMENT WITH THE DATE ON IT, A TINY VASE, BEDSIDE CLOCK OR A MUSIC BOX. ♥ CRYSTALS ARE BEAUTIFUL & PURPORTED TO TO BE MAGICAL. ♥

"It is good to be children sometimes, & never better than at Christmas."

♥ Charles Dickens ♥

RECIPE
FOR A
HAPPY CHRISTMAS
Fill a house with equal parts of Love, Hope, & Peace
Add the Joy of children, the Strength of older people, and the Spirit of Christ.
Spread over all the Blessings of Contentment.
Season with the music of Laughter & some Mistletoe Kisses
Warm before a crackling fire. Serve with Great Welcome, Much Cheer, and All the food in this book!
S.B.
XOXOXO
HO HO HO
"WITH POMP, POWER AND GLORY THE WORLD BECKONS VAINLY,
IN CHASE OF SUCH VANITIES WHY SHOULD I ROAM?
WHILE PEACE AND CONTENT BLESS MY LITTLE THATCHED COTTAGE,
AND WARM MY OWN HEARTH WITH THE TREASURES OF HOME."
BEATRIX POTTER

Have a Christmas Caroling Party — have everyone arrive early so you can sing a few rounds to practice. Ask your carolers to dress in their most colorful Christmas clothes, or you can set a theme by suggesting they wear Victorian, or something from A Christmas Carol — more ideas:

The words! You'll be surprised at how many words you have forgotten — so hand out typed sheets with the words to favorite carols.

Invite all ages — fun for older & younger & middle ones, too. Tie a wreath of aluminum stars around children's heads.

Have lots of extra mittens, hats & scarves on hand — & a Santa hat!

Carry a flashlight — put a fat candle in a jam jar, tie it to a stick to be carried ahead.

If hay wagons & horses are available — yes! Bring blankets, hot water bottles & don't forget the thermos.

Drop by a rest home — or the hospital. — Come home, all chilly & cold, to a winter picnic in front of the fire — toast marshmallows. ♥

THE FIREPLACE

In wintry places, the hearth is the natural gathering place for holiday celebrations — whether it be a festive tree trimming party, or just a cozy bowl of soup — in front of the fire is best. Keep your fire burning through the holiday season — it says welcome, come in, get warm! Here are some ideas:

The Yule Log: I love this because it's whimsical, traditional & solemn all at once. Two weeks before Christmas everyone goes out to the woodpile to choose the biggest, most beautiful log to burn on Christmas Eve. Carry it into the house where it can be tied with a red ribbon & decorated with sprigs of rosemary (the symbol of friendship & remembrance). If you don't have a fireplace, it can be drilled with a hole, filled with a candle, & decorated with soap snow (p.34). Display it on the hearth until Christmas Eve. Then, with great ceremony, burn the Yule Log (or light the candle) & all say a prayer to go up in the smoke. ♥

Fragrant Herb Bundles: After using the leaves of your summer herbs, collect all the woody stems from basil, rosemary, thyme, & marjoram. Cut them to a uniform length & tie into bundles with ribbon or string. When packed into a basket with tiny pinecones, the bundles make a sweet hearthside Christmas gift with a wonderful fragrance when burned. Save some for yourself!

Cinnamon Spice: Beribboned bundles of cinnamon sticks set near a warm fire will send off a delicious scent to fill the room with Christmas fragrance. ♥

Christmas Day

Christmas Day can go slow. I remember my uncles, one on each couch, asleep on Christmas Day. Now it's me! Here are some ideas for Christmas day ~ for fun, for relaxation, & for the memories.

- Give overnight guests a little breakfast in bed ~ some coffee & warm pumpkin bread with some red grapes is plenty. Put all on a tray with flowers, lace napkins ~ pamper them a little bit. ♥

- Give a fun Christmas gift that gets people outside during the day. Or, go for a walk & admire nature.

- Encourage people to "stop by" ~ it gives a nice break of new faces ~ stop by someone else's house ~ give them a break!

- Rent a movie (& a VCR) so there is something to veg-out on ~ while THEY'RE doing THAT ~ YOU can take a NAP ☺.

- If you invite someone to dinner, & if they want to bring something, say YES & suggest they bring whatever was traditional for them, at home. ♥

- Drag out dinner, eat slowly ~ linger at the table; pull out a book of carols at the end ~ sing them all ~ you'll be beautiful! Do "The Twelve Days of Christmas" ~ everybody take a part (or two). ♪

- Light candles, say a prayer holding hands, play music, dress up & take pictures, kiss everyone within 5 feet of the mistletoe, & keep your senses *alive* so you can remember THIS Christmas all year long. ♥

Main Dishes

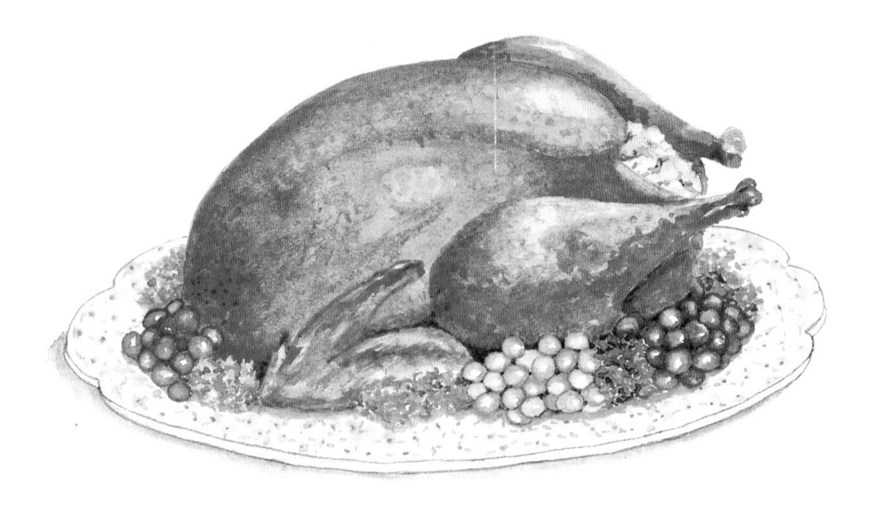

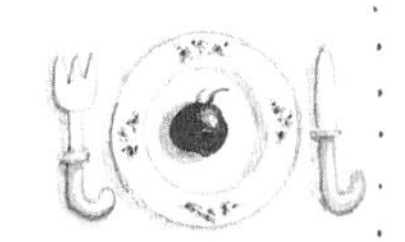

"Many merry Christmases, friendships,
great accumulation
of
cheerful recollections,
affection on earth,
and
Heaven at last for all of us."

♥ Charles Dickens

MOTHER'S GOOSE

450° Serves 6-8

Traditional roasted goose ~ so delicious with this beautiful orange-flavored sauce & very easy to make. A goose has a lot of fat on it which makes him a bad candidate for stuffing ~ it's OK. because you get rid of most of the fat during preparation & you can serve him with the delicious (baked in the oven) Wild Rice & Apples on p. 41. ♥

Basic Information: A 10 lb. bird serving 6-8 will cook for 2 hours, approx. 12 min. per pound. You will need a roasting thermometer, skewers, a basting bulb, & kitchen string. When you order your goose from the butcher, ask for a young, fresh one, although frozen is O.K. if slowly thawed in refrigerator. Save all the giblets ⟶ make the sauce as the goose is roasting. Goose must sit uncarved after roasting for 20 min. ~ so include in time schedule.

1 10 lb. young, gorgeous goose
1 lemon, salt
liver, giblets & neck of goose
2 Tbsp. reserved goose fat
1 small onion, diced
1 lg. carrot, chopped
1 lg. celery stalk, chopped
3 c. chicken broth (homemade, if you have it)
2 small bay leaves
goose roasting pan with brown bits, all fat removed
½ c. port wine
1½ Tbsp. cold water } mixed together till smooth
2 Tbsp. cornstarch }
1 orange peel, no pith, very thinly sliced
freshly cracked pepper

Preheat oven to 450°. Remove giblets & neck from body cavity & reserve. Pull out & discard visible lumps of fat (neck area, etc.). Rinse bird inside & out & pat dry. With a fork, prick skin at ½" intervals all around thighs & in lower breast area (so fat can drain). Pull neck skin over opening & fasten with skewer. Squeeze lemon juice over entire bird, & salt him lightly inside & out. Tie the drumsticks together with string. Place goose on wire rack in large roasting pan & roast 1 hr. at 450°, breast side down.

♥♥♥

Mother's Goose ♥♥♥

Every 30 min. during roasting, siphon off fat with basting bulb; the first time you do it, put 2 Tbsp. fat into 3 qt. saucepan & reserve for sauce. (As for the rest of the fat, it is flavorful & can be reserved & frozen in ice cube trays for later use in soups & sauces — or you can discard it.) After one hour, reduce heat to 325° & turn goose breast-side up. Insert roasting thermometer into thickest part of breast; do not touch bone. (At 175°, goose is done.) Roast 1 more hour (at 325°). If goose needs browning, turn heat to 400° for last 15 min. of cooking. You may show goose on a decorated platter if you like, but he is best carved into thin slices in the kitchen where you can discard skin & any fatty pieces. Allow whole goose to sit 20 min. before carving. Remove remaining fat from pan but save what's left, in the roasting pan, for the sauce.

Orange Sauce: Make this as goose is roasting. Finely dice the extremely flavorful & valuable goose liver & reserve in refrigerator. Dice giblets, break neck in half & place pieces in 3 qt. saucepan with 2 Tbsp. goose fat; brown on all sides. Add onion, carrot & celery pieces to pot; stir in broth & bay leaves. Cover & simmer while goose roasts (1½ hrs. or more). When goose is done & resting, pour the broth mixture into defatted roasting pan & scrape up brown bits. Pour this mixture through wire strainer back into sauce pan. Discard solids (or pick through for good stuff for kitty's Christmas dinner). Add diced liver to sauce & boil rapidly 2 min. Stir in port & bring back to boil. Whisk in cornstarch & water mixture — cook another minute, whisking. Remove from heat & immediately mix in 2 Tbsp. orange rind slivers (use the rest to garnish meat slices — a little sprinkling over all). Give the sauce a good grind of fresh cracked pepper to taste. Note: orange rind is easily done with sharp knife — white pith is nasty & bitter & will ruin everything it touches, don't let it get into your food. Cut the strips very thin, 1 to 1½ inches long.

TURKEYTALK TURKEYTALK TURKEYTALK TURKEYTALK TURKEYTALK TURKEYTALK TURKEYTALK

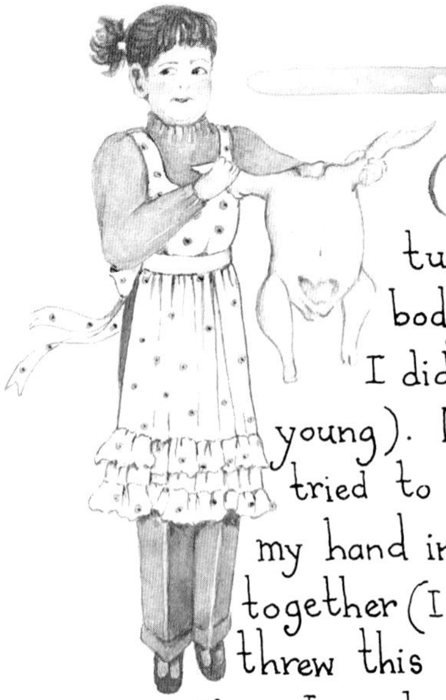

The first time I made a turkey, I found the neck in the body & had NO IDEA what it was. I didn't want to touch it (I was young). My mother wasn't home when I tried to get some advice — so I wrapped my hand in a dishtowel, squinched my eyes together (I didn't want to see it either) & threw this "body part" into the trash. Then I cooked the turkey, & along with it, the little bag of giblets in the neck cavity!

If your mother's not home, there's help: call the Turkey Hotline with your turkey trials & tribulations: 800/323-4848. They talk turkey talk. ♥

TURKEYTALK TURKEYTALK TURKEYTALK TURKEYTALK TURKEYTALK TURKEYTALK ♥

ROAST TURKEY

Make sure the turkey you buy will fit in your oven with roasting pan! Cook approx. 13 min. per pound if bird weighs 16 lbs. or less; 10 min. per pound if heavier. For a perfectly roasted bird, a meat thermometer is the very best measure. You will also need a basting bulb, skewers, & kitchen string. A 14 lb. bird will serve 8 & take about 3 hrs. to cook ~ so plan accordingly. The best is always fresh, unfrozen, & can be ordered from your butcher. The skin should have as few nicks & cuts as possible so juices will stay in ~ handle gently.

1 turkey	salt & pepper
1/2 c. butter, softened	stuffing

Heat oven to 450°. Remove neck & gizzards & save for gravy. Gently wash turkey inside & out & dry thoroughly with paper towels. Loosely stuff neck cavity & skewer skin closed. Stuff the rest of bird ~ skewer & tie legs tightly together over opening with string. Tuck wing tips underneath & toward center of bird. Rub softened butter all over bird ~ melt remaining butter for basting. Salt & pepper turkey & place breast down on rack in shallow roasting pan. Place in oven & turn temp. down to 350°. Baste every 20 min., first with melted butter & later with juices in bottom of pan. Turn turkey over after 1-1½ hrs. Tent with aluminum foil if bird begins to brown too much. Test with meat thermometer ~ remove turkey from oven when temp. registers 180° in thickest part of thigh ~ do not touch thermometer to bone. Place turkey on platter, cover loosely with towel & allow to sit at least 15 min. before carving. For stuffing & gravy, see pp. 54-55.

Mustard Roasted

LEG OF LAMB

450° Serves 8

Begin roasting at high temperature & what you'll have is juicy pink meat, slathered in spicy Dijon mustard & covered with a crunchy, toasted breadcrumb crust. Ask your butcher to bone the lamb as noted below. ♥

1 8-lb. fresh lamb leg, boned
1/2 c. olive oil
salt & freshly ground pepper
2 c. Country Style Dijon Mustard
1/2 loaf good quality white bread, in crumbs

Preheat oven to 450°. After boning you should have 3 main pieces of meat & some little pieces. Lightly rub olive oil over all & salt & pepper. Tuck any small pieces of meat inside of larger ones & roll up snugly into 3 separate pieces. Brush a heavy coat of mustard over first piece & press on a thick coat of fresh breadcrumbs. (Note: to prepare breadcrumbs, place coarsely chopped fresh bread in food processor ~ do not over-process ~ you want coarse, fairly large crumbs.) Repeat with remaining meat & place all on a rack in a shallow roasting pan. Roast at 450° for 10 min. ~ reduce heat to 350° & continue cooking approx. 1 hour, until meat thermometer reads 140°. The smaller pieces will be done first ~ do not overcook. Let meat sit 15 min. before slicing. ♥

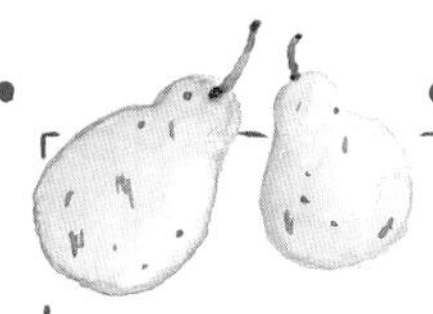

CRANBERRY CHICKEN & PEARS

Serves 4 to 6

Try this dish with the Sweet Potato Casserole on p. 49. Run a forkful of potatoes through this sauce (get some pear) ~ taste bud ecstasy. ♥

- ½ c. butter
- 2 lg. garlic cloves, minced
- 2 Tbsp. shallot, minced
- 4 whole chicken breasts, skinned, boned & halved ~ & floured
- 1 c. cranberries, coarsely chopped
- 4 ripe pears, peeled & sliced
- ⅔ c. brandy
- 1 c. heavy cream
- 1 c. sour cream
- ¼ c. parsley
- salt & freshly ground pepper, to taste

Melt half the butter in a lg. heavy skillet. Add garlic & shallot ~ cook 1 minute. Lightly flour chicken breasts & cook (in batches, using the rest of butter as needed) just until done, about 4 min. each side. Remove to platter & keep warm. Add cranberries to pan; cook & stir 1 min. Add pears & cook till slightly softened. Pour in brandy & flame, shaking pan till flame dies. Add creams, stir & heat through, don't boil. Taste & salt & pepper to taste. Pour sauce over breasts & sprinkle parsley over all. ♥ If you are careful not to overcook the chicken, this dish can be made ahead & rewarmed in a covered dish at low temp. in the oven; don't let the sauce bubble. ♥

TURKEY LASAGNA

375° Serves 10

A nice big family-style meal that takes the hurry out of Christmas. When I'm expecting an unknown number of guests I don't worry—make-ahead casseroles are the answer—and I spend my time talking to my friends

8 oz. lasagna noodles
1 lb. ground turkey
1 med. onion, chopped
2 cloves garlic, minced
1 16 oz. can peeled tomatoes, drained & chopped
8 oz. tomato sauce
6 oz. tomato paste
2 tsp. basil
1 tsp. oregano
½ tsp. thyme
2 tsp. fennel seed
¼ tsp. red pepper flakes
2 Tbsp. fresh parsley, minced
1 egg, beaten
2 c. low-fat cottage cheese
¼ tsp. freshly cracked pepper
¾ c. grated Parmesan cheese
8 oz. shredded, part skim milk mozzarella cheese

Lots of ingredients—easy to make. Preheat oven to 375°. Prepare noodles according to pkg. Rinse in cold water & set aside. In a skillet, cook turkey, onion, & garlic just until done. Stir in tomato products, dried seasonings, & 1 Tbsp. of the parsley. Simmer 15 min.; set aside. Meanwhile mix together egg, cottage cheese, pepper, ½ c. of the Parmesan, & the remaining Tbsp. of parsley. Set aside. To assemble: in a 9" x 13" baking dish layer half the noodles, half the cottage cheese mixture, half the meat mixture & half the mozzarella. Repeat layering with 2nd half of everything. Sprinkle with remaining ¼ c. of Parmesan. Bake 30 min., or cover & refrigerate & bake later.

"'For somehow, not only at Christmas, but all the long year through, the joy that you give to others is the joy that comes back to you."

♥ John Greenleaf Whittier

HONEY HAM

325° Serves 16~20

Delicious for a large party ~ perfect for a buffet.

1 10 lb. whole fully cooked ham
1 c. brown sugar
½ c. dry sherry
¼ c. honey
6 tbsp. Country Style Dijon mustard
½ tsp. freshly ground black pepper
½ fresh ripe pineapple, peeled, cored & thinly sliced
½ c. fresh cranberries

Preheat oven to 325°. Place ham on rack in roasting pan & bake 15 min. per pound, or about 2½ hours total. Combine sugar, sherry, honey, mustard & black pepper; set aside. After ham has cooked for 1¾ hrs., remove from oven, turn heat up to 425°. Pour juices from ham into shallow bowl; chill so that fat can be easily skimmed. Trim off excess fat from ham; score in ¾" diamond shapes with a sharp knife & coat generously with glaze. Turn oven back down to 325° & bake ham 15 min. ~ glaze again &, using toothpicks, decorate with pineapple & cranberries ~ return to oven 15 min. Once more, remove, glaze, & bake 15 min. Meat thermometer should read 135°~140°. Remove from oven, pour off juices & allow ham to sit 15~20 min. before slicing. Skim fat from pan juices ~ heat through & serve in gravy boat with sliced ham & cooked fruit.

CHRISTMAS EVE DINNER FEAST
STEAMED LOBSTERS

Casual, elegant, & romantic all at the same time — a colorful feast you eat with your hands. Invite best friends, have a Christmas stocking for each on the back of their chairs to open with dessert; candles, flowers, music & Christmas lights. As noted below, some recipes come from my other books, which make wonderful Christmas gifts.

Menu

Clams Casino (p. 18, Heart of the Home)
Steamed Lobsters (recipe below)
Steamed Mussels & Clams
Cherry Tomatoes Sautéed in Butter & Parsley
Roasted Green Beans (p. 72, Vineyard Seasons)
Big Bowl of Buttered Mashed Potatoes
Hot French Bread
Cherries Jubilee (p. 103, this book)

To cook lobsters: choose a 1½–2 lb. lobster per person. Put 1" water in a large pot with lid, add 1 Tbsp. vinegar (makes the shells bright red), bring to a boil. Drop in lobsters, cover & cook 18–20 min. Do not overcook; if you're unsure, take a lobster out of the pot & break off tail halfway — if the meat is white & opaque, it's done. Steam mussels & clams in water just until they open. Have the Clams Casino to start; pile unshelled lobster claws & tails into a large bowl and surround with clams & mussels; serve with lemon wedges & little bowls of melted butter. You'll need nutcrackers for the lobster shells & a big empty bowl for discarding shells in. Put the tomatoes & beans on another dish; bring out the bread & potatoes. A Feast! When it's all over & everyone is fat & happy, bring out a big bowl full of small hot towels for washing up. For dessert, Cherries Jubilee.

POACHED SALMON WITH LIME & GINGER SAUCE

Serves 6

So elegant & beautiful ~ serve with peas & Warm Spinach Salad (p. 53).

3 lbs. salmon filets
1/4 c. dry white wine
1/4 c. fresh lime juice
1 tsp. finely grated fresh ginger
1 1/2 c. cold butter

Boil 1" water in lg. skillet. Place salmon in pan; cover & gently poach till just cooked through. Meanwhile, boil wine, lime juice & ginger; reduce to 1-2 Tbsp. Turn heat very low. Whisking constantly, slowly add cold butter, 1 Tbsp. at a time. Pour sauce over salmon & serve.

ROAST PRIME RIBS OF BEEF

Roasting a standing rib roast couldn't be easier. To serve 10~12, have your butcher trim a 10 lb. standing rib roast. Preheat oven to 325°. Place meat, fat side up, in a shallow open pan. Roast for about 15 min. per lb., until meat thermometer registers 120° for rare; 140° for medium. Remove from oven & allow it to rest ½ hr. before slicing. Make some traditional Yorkshire Pudding & delicious Horseradish Sauce while meat rests ♥. So you know: you need approx 1 lb. meat per person (because of the bone) — if it's under 5 lbs. it roasts about 20 min. per lb. — if over 5 lbs., it's about 15 min. per lb. — a meat thermometer is a necessity.♥

YORKSHIRE PUDDING

6 Tbsp. drippings from roasting pan
3 eggs, beaten
1½ c. milk
1½ c. unbleached flour
1 tsp. salt

Turn oven to 450°. Pour pan drippings into a 9"x 13" pan — put the pan in the oven to get it hot. Beat eggs; gradually add in milk, flour, & salt, beating till well blended. Pour batter into hot pan & bake 25 ~ 30 min. Serve hot — good with roast juices♥

Horseradish Sauce

Mix together 2 c. sour cream, 4 Tbsp. horseradish, & salt & white pepper to taste. (Taste & add more horseradish if you like it.) Serve with beef.♥

WHISKEY STEAKS

Serves 6

The bourbon adds a wonderful flavor to this sauce. ♥

- 2 Tbsp. cooking oil
- 2 Tbsp. butter
- 6 ½-lb. beef tenderloins
- salt & freshly ground pepper
- 1 Tbsp. butter
- 2 Tbsp minced shallots
- ½ c. beef broth
- ⅓ c. bourbon
- 3 Tbsp. butter, softened

Heat oil & 2 Tbsp. butter over med. high heat. Sauté steaks 3–4 min. on each side for med. rare. Remove to a warm platter. Season with salt & pepper. Pour oil out of skillet; add 1 Tbsp. butter & the shallots — cook 1 min. Add beef broth & boil rapidly for 2 min., scraping pan. Add bourbon; boil 1–2 min. more. Remove from heat; stir in butter, a Tbsp. at a time. Pour sauce over steaks & serve. ♥

"It's love, it's love that makes the world go round."

from a French song

A Loss of Innocence

I was old when I found out about Santa Claus— I was twelve. At first I thought my mom kept it from me because she was afraid I'd tell the younger kids, but looking back, I think she just couldn't bear to break the news to me. I was such a staunch supporter of not only Santa, but the elves & reindeers, Rudolph & Mrs. Claus & the brownies, & everybody. I fixed special food for them every Christmas Eve & they ATE it. Proof positive. ♥

Then one November day there was a gang of neighborhood kids in our house arguing quite vocally about the non-existence of Santa Claus. I was shocked at how unbelievably dumb they could be, brazen morons really. I made it clear how I felt about their disloyalty & downright blasphemous attitudes: burnt cookies was all they'd be getting this Christmas. Of this, I was sure.

That evening my mother suggested we go for a ride in the car ALONE — unheard of in a family with 8 children. I knew something was up. But what?— what could it possibly be?

Staring out the window at the night stars, I listened quietly as she told me. After she finished there was a long silence, then my quivering voice asking "the Easter Bunny?" and she shook her head. Then the big one, the one I knew couldn't possibly be included in this hideous deception, "the Tooth Fairy?"

A Loss of Innocence . . .

All gone, swept away — all I had left were the princes & princesses (many of whom lived in trees in dark forests) in my fairy tale books, & I wasn't about to bring them up. I'd heard enough for one day.

Time has passed & I am a grownup now. The truth is that there ARE fairies & brownies; I don't care what anyone says. They live in the woods around my house, they keep fireflies as pets, & they help me write these books. Proof positive. ♥

CHRISTMAS CARDS & LETTERS

If you would like your Christmas cards to carry a more "authentic" postmark: address & put stamps on them; put them all in a large manila envelope & send it in care of the postmaster of one of these towns: North Pole, Alaska 99705; Santa Claus, Indiana 47579; or Christmas, Florida 32709. They will postmark your cards with the name of their town & send them out. Mail early!

Most post offices have "Santa's Elves" who personally answer children's letters to Santa — check with yours. Or, if you send them to North Pole, Alaska, they will be answered by the 6th & 7th grade writing classes at the North Pole Middle School. In Santa Claus, Indiana, there's an "elf" volunteer group to handle Santa's mail. On Martha's Vineyard we have Mr. Eddie Colligan, who takes the time to answer letters & grant the wishes of little ones. ♥

"... the French plums blushed in modest tartness from their highly decorated boxes."

Charles Dickens

DESSERTS

COOKIES
Candies
Cake
PIE
PUDDING

MUCH
MUCH
MORE

... In apple baskets, lined with paper doilies or with a clean, new dishtowel.

... In heart-shaped fabric-covered boxes,

or ... In old pottery bowls, wrapped in lace napkins & tied with ribbons.

... In small ice buckets,

... In sewing baskets, tin buckets, or spread on a pretty tray...

And they taste Just As Good in a brown paper bag tied with a Christmas ribbon!

Hand write the recipe on a card & tie it with ribbon or yarn to your cookie gift ♥.

Annie Hall's BUTTER COOKIES

350° Makes 6~8 dozen

When my friend Annie comes to dinner, her whole name is on her placecard — I just can't seem to resist! And she gave me this recipe for "the best butter cookie in the world today". (Well, we think so ♥.) You can do ANYTHING with it — twist into candy canes, roll out for cookie cutters, or drop into shapes — anything & everything & they taste fabulous ♥.

2 c. butter, softened
1½ c. sugar
4 egg yolks
2 tsp. vanilla
4½ c. unbleached flour
½ tsp. salt

Preheat oven to 350°. With an electric mixer (even the hand-held kind), cream together butter & sugar. Add egg yolks & vanilla & mix well. Sift flour & salt together & beat into butter mixture until well mixed. When ready to bake use an <u>ungreased</u> cookie sheet & place cookies 1" apart. Bake for about 10 minutes, but do not brown them. Remove cookies from cookie sheet while still warm & cool on sheets of waxed paper. Decorate, if you like ♡.

NEXT PAGE FOR COOKIE SHAPES:

Here's what you can do with Annie Hall's BUTTER COOKIE batter:

CANDY CANES: Divide 3c. of dough in half. Add 1½ tsp. red food coloring to one half. Using about a tablespoon of dough, roll a 4" strip of each color (no fatter than a pencil). Place the two colored rolls side-by-side & press lightly together. Gently twist like a rope & place on ungreased cookie sheet 1" apart. Curve the top like a candy cane & bake about 10 min.; do not brown. You can sprinkle with crushed peppermint candy, if you like.

Roll Cookies: Shape dough into rolls the width of a cookie. Wrap in waxed paper & chill. Before baking, roll in chocolate shots. Slice ½" thick & bake on ungreased cookie sheet at 350° for 10 min.; do not brown.

Stars, Hearts, Circles & Jelly-filled: Fill a pastry bag with unchilled dough & put through a "star tip" (sizes 2 & 7-9). Squeeze onto cookie sheet into the shapes you like ~ just a "bloop" to make "stars" ~ fill baked centers with red jelly. Decorate these cookies with cinnamon hearts, mini chocolate morsels, colored sugar, those little silver balls, or frosting from a tube (Dec a Cake®). Bake them, same as others. Do not brown.

Cookie Cutter Cookies: Chill dough. Roll out onto lightly floured board to thickness of ½". Cut with cookie cutters & bake as often mentioned above. Decorate in your own inimitable way ♥.

Plain Old Drop Cookies: Just drop unchilled dough by teaspoonfuls onto ungreased cookie sheet. Bake. 350°. 10 min. Don't brown. Remove from pans immediately. Eat.

CHRISTMAS WREATHS

Makes about 24

These are adorable — easy to make and look great on the cookie plate. The recipe is a version of the widely acclaimed Rice Krispie Treat.

36 lg. marshmallows
1/2 c. butter
1/2 tsp. vanilla
1/4 tsp. green food coloring
3 1/2 c. cornflakes
1 pkg. candy redhots

Over medium heat, melt marshmallows & butter together. Stir in vanilla & food coloring. Fold in cornflakes & mix well. Drop by tablespoonfuls onto waxed paper. Working quickly with buttered fingers, form into little wreaths. Decorate with candies. They will firm up as they cool.

"Best of all are the decorations the grandchildren have made — fat little stars and rather crooked Santas, shaped out of dough and baked in the oven."

Gladys Taber

Mary's Mother's SNOWBALLS

350° Makes 2½ dozen

A cookie with a surprise — it's wrapped around a Chocolate Kiss! Mary's mother is famous for her kisses ♥

2 sticks butter, softened
3/4 c. sugar
2 c. sifted flour
1 c. finely chopped walnuts
8 oz. Chocolate Kisses
powdered sugar, for dusting

Cream butter & sugar well, until smooth. Add flour, then walnuts. Gather dough into disk-shape & wrap in plastic. Refrigerate at least ½ hr. Preheat oven to 350°. Remove foil from Kisses & insert one inside a ball of dough 1" in diameter. Make sure each Kiss is completely covered by dough. Bake on ungreased baking sheet for about 12 min., until just cooked through. Sift over powdered sugar while still warm. ♥

"The ancient white house with its steep roof and low eaves looks like a ship anchored in a still, white sea."
♥ Gladys Taber

GRANDMA'S FROSTED MOLASSES COOKIES

350° Makes about 4½ doz.

A big, soft, old-fashioned cookie with a powdered sugar frosting.

- 1 c. sugar
- 1 c. butter, softened
- 1 c. molasses
- 1 c. sour cream
- 3 tsp. baking soda
- 3 Tbsp. white vinegar
- 2 tsp. ginger
- ½ tsp. salt
- 3 eggs, beaten
- 4 c. unbleached flour, sifted

Preheat oven to 350°. Cream butter & sugar well. Add molasses & sour cream ~ mix well. Mix the soda with the vinegar & add it along with ginger & salt. Stir in beaten eggs, then sifted flour. Drop by rounded tablespoonfuls onto greased cookie sheet 2" apart. Bake 10-12 min. Remove from pan & cool on sheets of waxed paper. Finished cookie should be about 3½" across. Frost.

Frosting

- 2 c. packed powdered sugar, sifted
- 5½ Tbsp. milk
- 2 tsp. butter

(milk and butter: heat together)

- 1 tsp. lemon extract
- 2-3 Tbsp. extra hot milk

With a wooden spoon beat sugar with hot milk & butter mixture. (Put extra milk on to heat.) Beat in extract. If necessary, add additional hot milk until creamy & spreadable. Work quickly & frost immediately. If frosting begins to harden, beat in another drop of hot milk. Frost thinly & let cookies dry before stacking.

"Star Light, Star Bright ~ First Star I see Tonight ~ Wish I May, Wish I Might ~ Have this Wish I Wish Tonight."

SNOWFLAKES

Makes about 24

So pretty—powdered-sugar-covered delicate snowflake-shaped cookies. You'll need to have a rosette maker, available at hardware or cooking equipment stores—not expensive & worth it so your party table can have real snowflakes on it. Kids love them; me too!

1 c. cornstarch
1/4 c. flour
4 tsp. sugar
2 tsp. freshly grated nutmeg
1 tsp. ground mace
rind of 2 lemons, grated
2 eggs
1/2 c. milk
1 qt. vegetable oil
powdered sugar

Mix together cornstarch, flour, sugar, nutmeg & mace. In another bowl, beat together grated lemon rind, eggs, & milk. Pour egg mixture into dry ingredients & mix till smooth. Heat vegetable oil to 375° on a deep-frying thermometer, maintain heat over med. high flame. For each cookie, preheat iron in oil, gently place iron into batter nearly to top—but not over the top. (If batter doesn't adhere, oil is either too hot or too cold.) Lower iron slowly into oil & cook about 7 seconds, till lightly golden. Remove from oil, gently loosen with fork tines & ease off onto paper towels. Sift over powdered sugar & serve immediately. If you want to use them later: make the snowflakes, do not sugar, allow to cool completely & store in airtight container. Just before serving, lay cookies on cookie sheet & reheat in preheated 350° oven for 2 min. Sift sugar over—put them on serving plate & eat ♥. It's sad, but once these cookies are sugared, they don't keep well; however, I think they're worth the trouble & are especially nice for a buffet. ♥

Holly

CHRISTMAS NUT COOKIES

300° Makes 9 dozen

My grandma says that I should say that these aren't JUST for "Christmas Nuts"—other people like them too! This delicious cookie travels well ~ she sends them to all the luckiest people.

1 1/2 c. unsalted butter, softened
1/4 c. Crisco, room temp.
3/4 c. sugar
1 c. finely chopped nuts (walnuts, almonds, or pecans)
2 tbsp. vanilla
4 c. unbleached, unsifted flour
powdered sugar, to roll in (not you ~ the cookies!) (OH WELL, IT'S CHRISTMAS—GO AHEAD.)

Cream butter, Crisco & sugar together. Add other ingredients (except powdered sugar). Be sure to work in all the flour, use your hands. Roll into a large ball, wrap in plastic wrap & refrigerate several hours or overnight. Before baking, allow the dough to sit at room temp. till just soft enough to handle ~ about 1/2 hr. Preheat oven to 300°. Roll into small walnut-sized balls; place on ungreased cookie sheet 1" apart. Turn oven down to 275°, bake for 30~35 min. ~ they should be VERY light colored. Cool 15 min., then roll in powdered sugar. My grandma says to roll them again in powdered sugar before packing in boxes to mail.

Chocolate Dipped Coconut Macaroons

325° Makes about 30

Elegant-looking chewy coconut confections edged in semi-sweet chocolate. Easy to make. ♥

2 2/3 c. flake coconut, firmly packed
2/3 c. sugar
1/4 c. unbleached flour
4 egg whites, unbeaten
1 c. sliced almonds
1 tsp. vanilla extract
1 tsp. almond extract

8 oz. semi-sweet chocolate, coarsely chopped

Preheat oven to 325°. Combine coconut, sugar & flour. Stir in egg whites, almonds, vanilla & almond extract. Form balls from rounded tablespoonfuls & place 2" apart on lightly greased cookie sheets. Bake 20-25 min. until golden. Remove from pans while hot & allow to cool. ♥ Chocolate Edge: Melt chocolate in double boiler, stirring until 2/3 melted; remove from heat & continue stirring until completely melted. Dip one edge of each cookie into chocolate & set on wax paper to allow chocolate to set. ♥

"Chill December brings the sleet,
Blazing fire and Christmas treat."

Mother Goose ♥

Florentine Cookies

350° Makes about 40

WAY better than store-bought. Make your own Candied Orange Peel (good in so many Christmas recipes, see pg. 91) & you won't believe the difference ♥.

½ c. sugar
½ c. heavy cream
1¼ c. sliced almonds
¼ c. candied orange peel, finely chopped & homemade (p. 91)
¼ c. candied citron, finely chopped

1 Tbsp. unsalted butter
3 Tbsp. flour
½ tsp. almond extract

5 oz. semi-sweet chocolate

Preheat oven to 350°. Line a cookie sheet with foil & butter it well. (If you have parchment paper, use it ~ no need to butter.) In a heavy saucepan bring the sugar & cream to boiling point ~ reduce heat & simmer 3 min., stirring. Add all other ingredients except chocolate &, stirring constantly, cook over low heat for 3 more minutes. Spoon mixture by rounded teaspoons onto cookie sheets ~ 2½" apart ~ they spread. Bake 8~10 min. until golden. Using a round cookie cutter (they are very hot) reshape cookies into circles by gently pressing in edges. Slide foil off pan & cool completely. Melt chocolate in double boiler & cool slightly. Spread a thin layer of chocolate on the smooth side of each cookie (the bottom). Immediately draw fork tines through the chocolate in an "S" pattern. Set cookies, chocolate side up, in a cool place till chocolate sets. Can be stored in an airtight container with waxed paper between layers for up to 2 weeks. ♥

COOKIES

Candied ORANGE PEEL

Makes 1 cup

This works with all citrus & you can double this recipe so you'll have extra around to add to all sorts of Christmas recipes. It's delicious in stuffings, cookies, muffins, vegetables — anywhere you want the delicious surprise of bittersweet orange.

1 c. peel (about 1½ oranges)
1/4 c. water
1/2 c. sugar

Score oranges in quarters & remove peel. Scrape a sharp knife over skin to release oils. Cut into small squares; put in small heavy saucepan with enough cold water to cover. Bring to a boil, reduce heat & simmer 10 min. Drain, rinse & repeat this boiling, simmering & rinsing process 2 more times — this takes most of the bitterness from the peel. Add 1/4 c. water plus the sugar to the peel; slowly bring to boil, stirring until sugar dissolves — reduce to simmer, watching closely until syrup is almost absorbed, stir gently until completely absorbed. Pour out onto oiled (vegetable) surface to cool & dry somewhat. Store in an airtight container in freezer or refrigerator.

RUM TRUFFLES

Makes about 24

These are particularly rich & chocolatey — & extremely easy to make.

5 oz. unsweetened chocolate, chopped
2½ c. powdered sugar, sifted
1 stick unsalted butter, at room temperature
4 tsp. dark rum
unsweetened cocoa (for rolling truffles in), sifted

Melt chocolate over very low heat in a heavy saucepan. Remove from heat; stir in sugar & butter, a little at a time. Add rum & beat well. Roll into walnut-sized balls (or smaller if you like); place on waxed paper to cool completely. Roll in cocoa powder. Serve at room temp.

HOT ALMOND CRUNCH

6 Servings

Delicious served over softened vanilla ice cream.

3 Tbsp. unsalted butter
1 c. slivered almonds, coarsely chopped
1/3 c. light brown sugar, packed

Have all ingredients measured & ready to go — soften ice cream. In a heavy skillet, melt butter; add almonds, shaking & stirring till lightly toasted. Add sugar & stir vigorously till melted — be careful not to burn. Spoon over ice cream & serve.

"HEAP ON MORE WOOD! — THE WIND IS CHILL;
BUT LET IT WHISTLE AS IT WILL,
WE'LL KEEP OUR CHRISTMAS MERRY STILL."

Sir Walter Scott

CARAMEL APPLES

Makes 10

Old-fashioned delicious Christmas treats; use the crispest, juiciest apples you can find.

2 14-oz. pkgs. candy caramels
4 Tbsp. water
10 apples, McIntosh, Granny Smith, Delicious
wooden sticks

In a heavy pan, over low heat, melt caramels with water. Stir occasionally till smooth. Wash & dry apples, remove stems & insert sticks in stem end. Dip apples in melted caramel; scrape excess from bottom. Place on parchment paper or buttered waxed paper. Chill to set.

POPCORN BALLS

Makes 8

A basket of Caramel Apples & Popcorn Balls all tied up in ribbons looks wonderful — these buttery-sweet balls taste great!

8c. popped corn (1/2 c. unpopped)
1/2 c. light corn syrup
1/2 c. water
1 tsp. white vinegar
1/4 tsp. salt
3/4 c. brown sugar
3/4 c. white sugar
3/4 c. butter

Put popped corn in lg. bowl. Combine all remaining ingredients, except butter, in a saucepan. Heat to boiling over med. high heat, stirring often. Cook, stirring constantly, to 260° on candy thermometer. Remove from heat, stir in butter till melted — slowly pour over popcorn, stirring to coat. Cool slightly — butter hands, shape into 3" balls & place on waxed paper.

In Ice Cream...

Chocolate Poached Pears

Serves 6

1 c. sugar
2 c. water
1 c. white sherry
½ vanilla bean, split lengthwise
juice of one lemon
6 ripe Bosc pears, peeled, cored, leaving stem intact
1½ pts. vanilla ice cream, softened
Chocolate Sauce (below)

In a 4 qt. non-aluminum pan, combine sugar, water, sherry, vanilla bean & lemon juice; bring to simmer over med. low heat. Peel, & core the pears from the bottom; leave stems on. Arrange the pears in the simmering syrup so that they are not pressed too tightly together. Cover & poach 15~25 min., until tender, but still fairly firm when pierced. Chill pears in liquid, basting occasionally. Just before serving, make Chocolate Sauce.

Chocolate Sauce

1½ tbsp. unsalted butter
2 oz. unsweetened chocolate
⅓ c. boiling water
¾ c. sugar
3½ tbsp. corn syrup
½ tsp. vanilla extract

Melt butter & chocolate in a heavy saucepan over low heat; add boiling water & stir well. Stir in sugar & corn syrup till smooth. Boil 10 min. without stirring. Remove from heat; allow to cool 10 min. Stir in vanilla. While chocolate is cooling, let ice cream soften. Scoop ice cream onto dessert dish ~ set a pear on top & drizzle over warm chocolate sauce ... mmmm ... serve.

Pots de Crème

Serves Four

Smooth, rich chocolate ~ fast & easy, made in the blender or food processor ~ serve in little pots or in glass goblets. ♥ We took a trayful of them to a party; everyone loved them!

- 3/4 c. whole milk
- 6 oz. semi-sweet chocolate, chopped fine
- 1 lg. egg
- 2 Tbsp. sugar
- 1 tsp. vanilla
- pinch of salt
- 3 Tbsp. rum
- whipped cream

Heat milk slowly, just to boiling point. Put all other ingredients <u>except</u> rum & whipped cream into blender or food processor ~ slowly add hot milk & blend for 30 seconds. Add rum & continue blending 1 more minute. Pour into serving dishes; chill. Serve with a dollop of whipped cream. ♥

CROQUEMBOUCHE

375° Serves about 12

Such a gorgeous dessert — you say it "croak-em-boosh" — you'll need a pastry bag with a 1/4" tip to fill the tiny puffs with whipped cream. ♥

PUFFS

1 1/4 c. water
1/2 c. + 2 Tbsp. butter
1 1/4 c. flour
5 eggs at room temp.

2 c. cream whipped stiff with sugar & vanilla, to taste

Preheat oven to 375°. Boil water & butter together. Remove from heat, add flour all at once beating rapidly till dough forms a ball. (If it doesn't, put it back over med. heat & keep beating.) Cool 7 min. Add eggs, one at a time, beating frantically after each till dough is smooth. Butter & flour cookie sheets & drop by small teaspoonfuls 2" apart & bake 16 min. till brown & puffed. Put a little slit in each one, put them back in oven for 10 min. more. Cool completely. Fill them from bottom with whipped cream. Refrigerate till ready to assemble. Make the caramel & pile puffs into a pyramid using caramel as "glue" — dip bottoms. Make the chocolate & dribble it over all. ♥

Caramel

1 c. sugar & 1/3 c. water

Bring to a simmer — swirl pan till sugar dissolves. Cover, bring to boil — when bubbles are thick, uncover & swirl till light brown — remove from heat. ♥

Chocolate

6 oz. semi-sweet choc.
& 4 Tbsp. butter

Stir constantly over low heat till melted. Sauce will harden as it cools. ♥

Serves 10–12

This traditional Christmas dessert is most often served from a large glass footed bowl – so you can see all the goodies inside.

- 1 pound cake
- about 1 c. raspberry jam
- 1 c. toasted almond slices
- 3/4 c. Harveys Bristol Cream
- 1/4 c. good quality Cognac
- 2 12-oz. pkgs. frozen raspberries, thawed & drained
- Vanilla Custard (below)
- 2 c. heavy cream, whipped with sugar & vanilla to taste
- a few sliced almonds, raspberries & strawberries to decorate top of Trifle

Slice cake into 1½" slices. Spread jam between 2 slices, put them together, continue with rest of cake. Cut the slices into 1" "fingers" – to fit bowl, & line it closely. Sprinkle over almond slices – pour over sherry & Cognac. Drain raspberries & make the Custard. Put the raspberries over the cake, pour on the cooled Custard & chill thoroughly – 4 to 5 hrs. When ready to serve, top with whipped cream; decorate with almonds & fruits.

Vanilla Custard

- 1½ Tbsp. cornstarch
- 2 c. whole milk
- 4 egg yolks
- ½ c. sugar
- 1½ tsp. vanilla

In a small bowl, mix together cornstarch & 1/4 c. of the milk. Beat yolks till light & combine with cornstarch mixture. Heat remaining milk in a saucepan – do not boil. Stir sugar into milk until dissolved. Very slowly, stir about 1 c. hot milk into egg yolks – then return all to saucepan. Stir constantly over low heat – about 10 min., till slightly thickened. Remove from heat; stir in vanilla. Cool to room temp., covered with plastic wrap.

FATHER'S BREAD PUDDING with WHISKEY SAUCE

325° Serves 12

1 lg. loaf day-old French bread, cut into 3/4" cubes, about 12 c.
3 eggs
2 c. milk
3 Tbsp. vanilla extract
1 c. sugar
3/4 tsp. cinnamon
3/4 tsp. nutmeg
3 c. peeled, sliced tart apples
1 c. cranberries, washed & lightly dusted with sugar

Topping
3/4 c. butter, cut into bits
3 Tbsp. cinnamon
2 tsp. nutmeg

Preheat oven to 325°. Butter 9" × 13" baking dish. Put bread into a large colander—pour about 4c. hot tap water over bread evenly. Allow to sit 5 min.—press out excess water & set aside. In a very lg. bowl, whisk together eggs, milk, vanilla, sugar & spices. Gently fold in bread, apples & cranberries. Pour into prepared dish. Drop butter bits evenly over the top. Mix together cinnamon & nutmeg—sprinkle over pudding. Bake 1 hr. & 20 min. Serve warm with hot whiskey sauce. Can be made ahead & baked later. ♥

Whiskey Sauce

1 c. butter
1 c. sugar
½ c. whiskey
2 eggs, beaten

Melt butter over med. heat. Add sugar, stir constantly till bubbly—about 2 min. Remove from heat & slowly stir in whiskey—continue cooking & stirring 1 min. Remove from heat & *slowly* add enough whiskey mixture to eggs to warm them, stirring briskly. Over low heat, stirring, add eggs to whiskey mixture—it will thicken. Serve. ♥ Can be gently rewarmed.

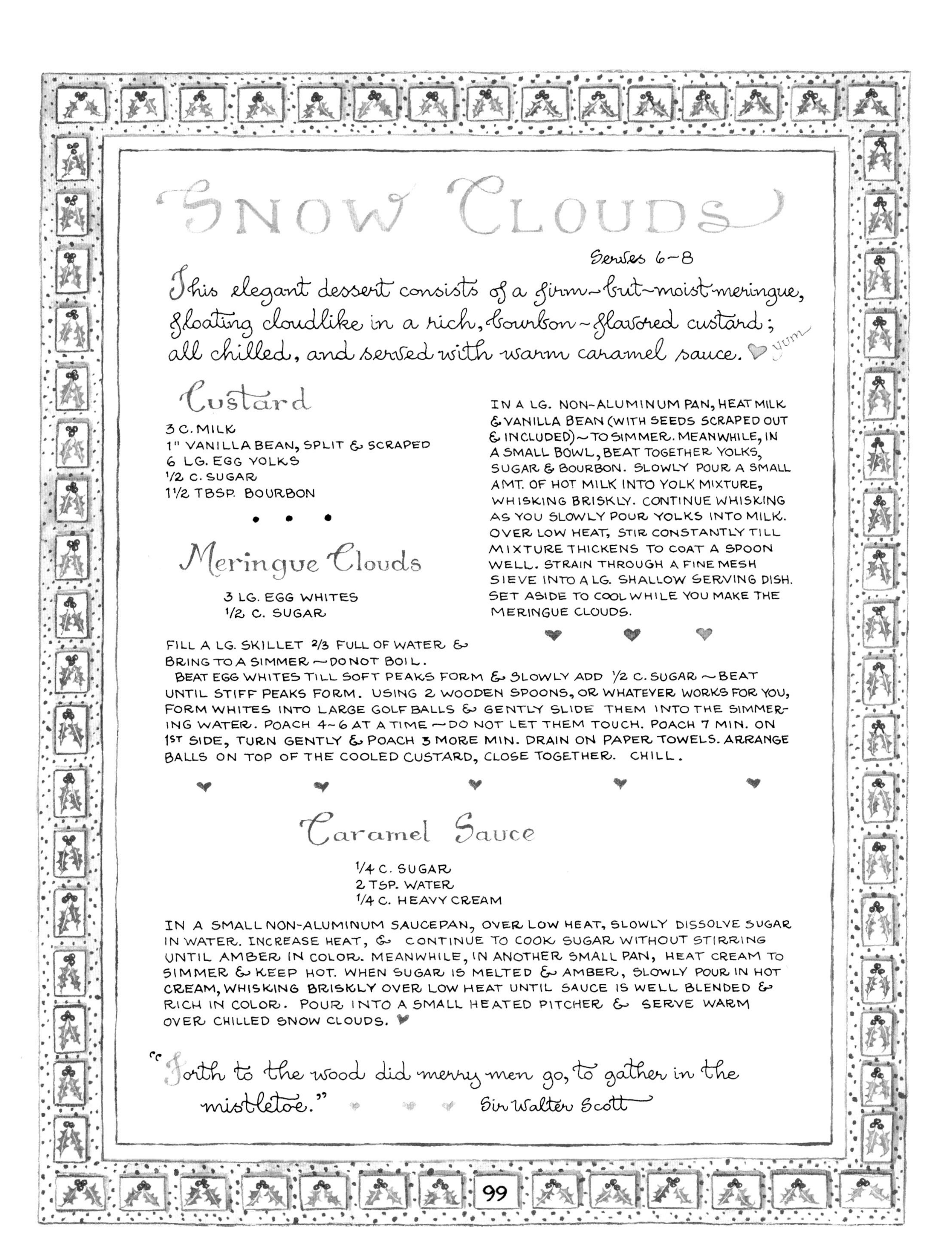

Snow Clouds

Serves 6–8

This elegant dessert consists of a firm-but-moist meringue, floating cloudlike in a rich, bourbon-flavored custard; all chilled, and served with warm caramel sauce. ♥ yum

Custard

3 C. MILK
1" VANILLA BEAN, SPLIT & SCRAPED
6 LG. EGG YOLKS
1/2 C. SUGAR
1 1/2 TBSP. BOURBON

IN A LG. NON-ALUMINUM PAN, HEAT MILK & VANILLA BEAN (WITH SEEDS SCRAPED OUT & INCLUDED) ~ TO SIMMER. MEANWHILE, IN A SMALL BOWL, BEAT TOGETHER YOLKS, SUGAR & BOURBON. SLOWLY POUR A SMALL AMT. OF HOT MILK INTO YOLK MIXTURE, WHISKING BRISKLY. CONTINUE WHISKING AS YOU SLOWLY POUR YOLKS INTO MILK. OVER LOW HEAT, STIR CONSTANTLY TILL MIXTURE THICKENS TO COAT A SPOON WELL. STRAIN THROUGH A FINE MESH SIEVE INTO A LG. SHALLOW SERVING DISH. SET ASIDE TO COOL WHILE YOU MAKE THE MERINGUE CLOUDS.

• • •

Meringue Clouds

3 LG. EGG WHITES
1/2 C. SUGAR

♥ ♥ ♥

FILL A LG. SKILLET 2/3 FULL OF WATER & BRING TO A SIMMER — DO NOT BOIL.

BEAT EGG WHITES TILL SOFT PEAKS FORM & SLOWLY ADD 1/2 C. SUGAR — BEAT UNTIL STIFF PEAKS FORM. USING 2 WOODEN SPOONS, OR WHATEVER WORKS FOR YOU, FORM WHITES INTO LARGE GOLF BALLS & GENTLY SLIDE THEM INTO THE SIMMERING WATER. POACH 4-6 AT A TIME — DO NOT LET THEM TOUCH. POACH 7 MIN. ON 1ST SIDE, TURN GENTLY & POACH 3 MORE MIN. DRAIN ON PAPER TOWELS. ARRANGE BALLS ON TOP OF THE COOLED CUSTARD, CLOSE TOGETHER. CHILL.

♥ ♥ ♥ ♥ ♥

Caramel Sauce

1/4 C. SUGAR
2 TSP. WATER
1/4 C. HEAVY CREAM

IN A SMALL NON-ALUMINUM SAUCEPAN, OVER LOW HEAT, SLOWLY DISSOLVE SUGAR IN WATER. INCREASE HEAT, & CONTINUE TO COOK SUGAR WITHOUT STIRRING UNTIL AMBER IN COLOR. MEANWHILE, IN ANOTHER SMALL PAN, HEAT CREAM TO SIMMER & KEEP HOT. WHEN SUGAR IS MELTED & AMBER, SLOWLY POUR IN HOT CREAM, WHISKING BRISKLY OVER LOW HEAT UNTIL SAUCE IS WELL BLENDED & RICH IN COLOR. POUR INTO A SMALL HEATED PITCHER & SERVE WARM OVER CHILLED SNOW CLOUDS. ♥

"Forth to the wood did merry men go, to gather in the mistletoe." ♥ ♥ ♥ Sir Walter Scott

CRÈME de PUMPKIN

325° Serves 6

I can't say enough nice things about this dessert. It is nothing like pumpkin pie, but the most creamy, smooth, delicious pudding-like confection with a snappy crust of caramelized brown sugar on the top.

3 c. heavy cream
6 egg yolks
1 can pumpkin puree (about 2 c.)
1/2 c. lt. brown sugar
5 tsp. vanilla extract
1/4 tsp. ground allspice
1 tsp. ground cloves
1/4 tsp. freshly ground nutmeg
3/4 c. dark brown sugar (for topping)

(Boil a teapotful of water to use later.) Preheat oven to 325°. Bring cream to boil over medium heat. Meanwhile whisk egg yolks into pumpkin, one at a time. Slowly whisk in lt. brown sugar, then vanilla & spices. When cream has reached boiling point, slowly pour into pumpkin mixture, whisking vigorously. Set an 8" square baking pan into a larger pan & pour the pumpkin mixture into the smaller pan. Place pans into upper half of oven & pour enough boiling water into larger pan to come up half way. Bake 1 hr. to 1 hr. & 10 min. till top is set ~ it will firm as it cools. Remove from water bath ~ made easier by siphoning off the water with a baster. Cover & chill thoroughly. Heat broiler. Sift brown sugar evenly & loosely over the top of pudding ~ set 5"-6" under broiler flame ~ WATCH CLOSELY; rotate often. In only 2-3 min. the sugar will liquefy & caramelize but it will also burn easily (so don't go off to fold the laundry). Serve, or chill first, uncovered. (I love it both ways, but chilled is my favorite.)

LEMON SQUARES

350° Makes 9 squares

This recipe helped me get my Girl Scout cooking badge (pictured above: the "credential" that still hangs on my studio wall) — it was the hit of all bake sales! Delicious!

- 1/2 c. unsalted butter, softened
- 1 c. unbleached flour
- 1/4 c. powdered sugar
- 1/4 tsp. lemon extract
- pinch of salt

Preheat oven to 350°. Thoroughly butter an 8" square pan. With an electric mixer, cream all ingredients till soft & smooth. (Or, in a food processor, till it forms a ball.) Press dough evenly into pan & bake 20 min. Meanwhile, make the topping.

- 2 eggs
- 1 c. sugar
- 1/4 tsp. lemon extract
- juice & zest of 1 lemon
- 1/4 c. unbleached flour
- 1/2 tsp. baking powder
- powdered sugar

With electric mixer, beat eggs well & gradually add sugar, until mixture is thick. Gradually add remaining ingredients, except powdered sugar. Continue beating till crust comes out of oven. Pour lemon mixture over hot crust, return it to oven & reduce heat to 325°. Bake 30-35 min. till top is golden. Remove from oven & run a sharp knife around the edge. Cool 20 min.; cut into squares, remove from pan & sift over powdered sugar. This recipe is easily doubled — use juice of 2 lemons but zest from only 1. Second baking time should be increased 3-5 min.

STEAMED CHRISTMAS PUDDING

Serves 12

1 c. + 2 Tbsp. sweet butter
2¼ c. flour
1 c. sugar
1 c. fresh bread crumbs
½ tsp. salt
1 tsp. baking powder
½ tsp. cinnamon
½ tsp. cloves
½ tsp. nutmeg

1 c. tart apple, peeled, cored & chopped med.
½ c. golden raisins, plumped in hot water & drained
½ c. dried apricots, chopped med.
1 c. dates, coarsely chopped
1 c. walnuts, coarsely chopped
1 c. buttermilk
½ c. unsulphered molasses
2 lg. eggs
1 Tbsp. vanilla

Use the 2 Tbsp. butter to coat the inside of a 2½ qt. pudding bowl or casserole & a piece of heavy foil cut 1" larger than diameter of bowl. Cut the rest of the butter into next 8 ingredients with a pastry cutter. Stir in fruits & nuts; add remaining ingredients & mix well. Pour into prepared bowl, cover with foil (buttered side down) & tie foil down tightly with string. Place on a rack in a deep kettle with 2" water in bottom. Cover, bring to a boil; reduce to simmer & steam 3½ hours (check water level periodically). Test with wooden skewer through foil. Cool 5 min.; invert onto serving plate & continue to cool 15–20 min. Serve with whipped cream or hard sauce. ♥

Hard Sauce

Process together: 1 c. softened sweet butter, 1½ c. powdered sugar, 1 egg yolk, ¼ c. heavy cream & ¼ c. cognac — till smooth & creamy. Serve at room temperature. ♥

Cherries Jubilee

Serves 6

Hot, brandied cherries poured over vanilla ice cream— wonderful because you can keep the ingredients on hand & be ready for a surprise dessert. ♥

¼ c. sugar
dash salt
1½ Tbsp. cornstarch
2 cans (16½ oz. each) pitted dark sweet cherries in syrup
4 Tbsp. brandy
1½ pts. good vanilla ice cream

In a large skillet mix together sugar, salt & cornstarch; add syrup from cherries, but reserve cherries for later. Bring to a boil, stirring constantly until thickened. Reduce heat to simmer & gently stir in cherries. Warm the brandy, ignite it & pour over cherries. Scoop ice cream into dessert dishes & pour hot cherries over. ♥

"The days are short, the weather's cold,
by tavern fires tales are told."

New England Almanac, Dec. 1704

♥ IDEAS FOR COLLECTIONS ♥

• BUNNIES & EGGS

• WOODEN SPOONS

• CHILDREN'S DISHES USE FOR BREAKFAST •

• CHILDREN'S CHAIRS •

OLD BOXES

• FEATHERED FRIENDS •

• SPOTTED DOGS

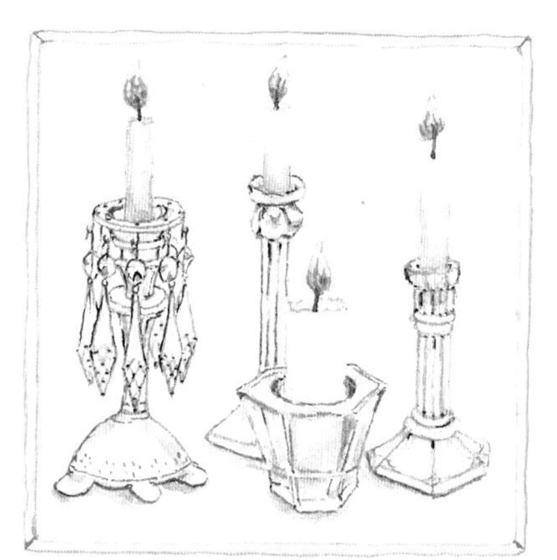

• CANDLE HOLDERS •

TEACUPS •

START A COLLECTION OF YOUR OWN, THEN EVERY-ONE WILL KNOW WHAT YOU WANT FOR CHRISTMAS ♥.

Baked Christmas Decorations

325°

Fun for everyone – easy to do. ♥

Ingred: 4 c. flour, 1 c. salt, about 1½ c. water.

Mix together flour & salt. Add water – dough should be stiff, not sticky. Knead 3–4 min.; if dough seems soft, knead in more flour. Make decorations – in shapes of wreaths, snow men, candy canes, Santas – & angels. Dip a finger in water to "glue" pieces together. Use sharp knives, fork tines & toothpicks to help make the decorations. Wrap thin wire around a pencil to make a hanger – twist ends & stick into dough. Bake on foil-lined cookie sheets 1 hr. at 325°. Remove; cool. Paint with watercolors. Bake again for 15 min. Paint or dip in polyurethane or clear nail polish if you wish them to keep. ♥

Dough can be rolled into round shapes or oblongs; it can be flattened or twisted – & even the tiniest pieces keep their shapes when baked. ♥

ANGEL BABIES

CHRISTMAS SHOPPING

"The best gifts are tied with heartstrings."

WHAT HAPPENS TO PEOPLE WHO WAIT TILL THE LAST MINUTE TO SHOP?

1. They spend the entire Christmas season at, what feels like, work. Hurrying (as opposed to "bustling"); no time to stop and smell the poinsettias ♥.

2. They buy the first thing they see, or "the last resort" which often turns out to be something yukky & boring, taking the fun of giving out of the season. (Plain pitiful.)

3. To top it off, they often spend too much money (being in such a hurry) and are still paying for Christmas in April!

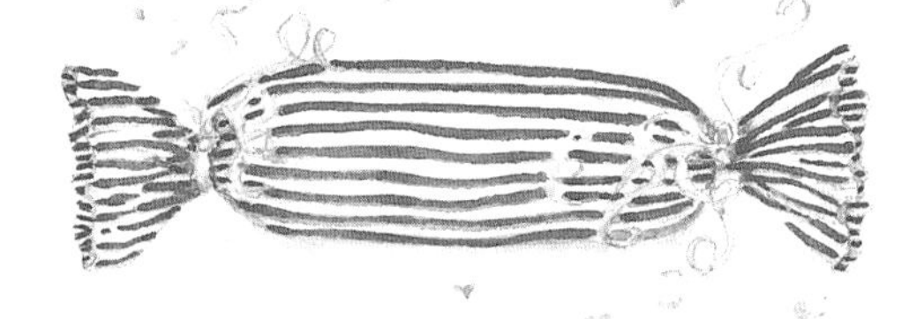

NO WONDER THERE ARE HUMBUGS!

Shop all year long. As you thumb through catalogs or walk through the mall, keep friends & family in mind. By Christmas you'll have a closet full of wonderful, thoughtful gifts. Instead of fighting crowds, feeling STRESS, you'll have time for visiting, playing with your children, tea time, celebrations & the spirit of Christmas. Even breakfast in bed. SLEEP. SMILING. ♥

THE GREAT ESCAPE

My grandma is a very light sleeper — and she slept with me in my bed on Christmas Eve. Extremely inconvenient for, as much as I loved her, I had only one thing on my mind between 4 a.m. & 6 a.m. Christmas morning & that was getting OUT of that bed & IN to the living room.

And so, very early one Christmas morning I decided I would REALLY try this time. Very slowly (it must have taken hours) I got parts of my body out of the bed. Inching my way & barely breathing, first a leg, then an arm, then the tiniest movements to get the middle of my body out — it was going extremely well! Extra carefully I slid out another leg — finally, only one arm to slowly drag across the bed to freedom. At the last possible moment, my grandma, quick as a lightning bolt, reached out, grabbed my arm & said, "Where are you going?" She scared the daylights out of me & that was the end of my "flight" — back to bed I went to wait for a more "appropriate" time for rising (like maybe dawn). Fortunately my brothers & sisters were in the same frame of mind as myself, but without the "bed guard" that had been set upon me — so it wasn't long till the tip-toe of little feet was heard in the hall, & I was set free! And I decided that next year I'd be the "bed guard" & sleep with the baby! ♥

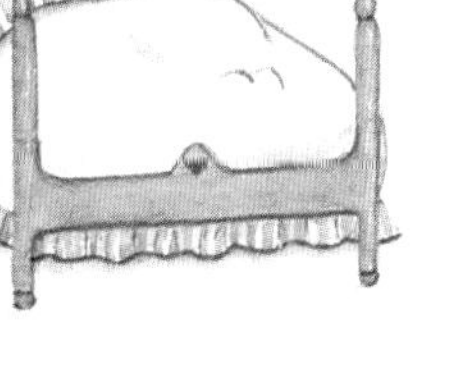

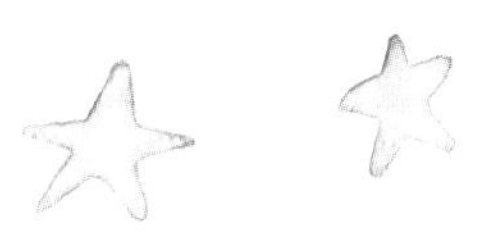

TEDDY BEAR TEA PARTY

This is darling at Christmas; a food-ladened table, surrounded with well-dressed Teddy bears enjoying their own Christmas party. I'm always on the lookout for tiny tea things, little flowered plates & napkins; special bear clothes made of linen & lace, straw hats & tiny Christmas jewelry — one of my bears has a pair of antique eye glasses. You can go as far as you want with it, and the collecting is so much fun. Silver salt spoons are perfect for stirring at this party — a frosted cookie, cut in wedges, makes a nice Teddy bear serving. The style can be Country or Victorian; either way, it's adorable — and you can do it too ♥.

Breakfast and Brunch

"Come in the evening, come in the morning,
Come when expected, come without warning;
Thousands of welcomes you'll find here before you,
And the oftener you come, the more we'll adore you."
Irish Rhyme

LITTLE-KNOWN CHRISTMAS SUPERSTITIONS THAT REALLY WORK

IF A GIRL SCOUT COMES TO YOUR DOOR ANYTIME IN DECEMBER, BUY WHAT SHE HAS GOT. SHE IS AN ANGEL IN DISGUISE.

DEC. 15TH, KISS A POMEGRANATE, ALL XMAS WISHES COME TRUE.

LISTEN TO "I'LL BE HOME FOR CHRISTMAS" 3 TIMES IN A ROW, AND YOU WILL BE. (IF NOT, TRY CLICKING YOUR HEELS TOGETHER 3 TIMES.)

DROP A SHELLED NUT IN ONE OF A TRAY OF CHRISTMAS CIDER MUGS — WHOEVER CHOOSES IT WILL PLAY A BIG ROLE IN YOUR LIFE.

DRAW A HEART IN PENCIL ON A PLAIN PIECE OF PAPER; SEND IT TO THE ONE YOU LOVE ON DEC. 21st HE WILL BE YOURS.

DURING THE CHRISTMAS SEASON OF YOUR 16TH YEAR IF A BABY SMILES AT YOU ~ TRUE LOVE IS NEAR BY.

CHRISTMAS

LOVE

DROP 3 CRANBERRIES ON THE GROUND ~ THE FURTHEST ONE OUT DIRECTS YOU TO THE ONE YOU LOVE. (DROP WITH A CERTAIN FLAMBOYANCE.)

IF YOU FIND AN ORANGE IN THE TOE OF YOUR CHRISTMAS STOCKING, VALENTINE'S DAY WILL BE GLORIOUS (AS OPPOSED TO CHRISTMAS :)

HARD BOIL AN EGG CHRISTMAS MORNING, IF IT CRACKS YOU WIN YOUR HEART'S DESIRE. (TIP: DROP ICE COLD EGG IN BOILING WATER.)

PULL OUT A GRAY HAIR ON CHRISTMAS DAY AND A CHILD WILL KISS YOU. POSSIBLY ALL DAY LONG.

ON CHRISTMAS EVE PUT THREE PINK PEPPERCORNS UNDER YOUR LOVER'S PILLOW; HE WILL DO THE CHRISTMAS DISHES.

THE BIG BOOK OF WELL-KNOWN FACTS

SMELL A YELLOW ROSE THE MORNING OF THE 17TH OF DEC. & THERE'S A GOOD CHANCE YOU'LL GET DIAMONDS FOR XMAS. (WELL-KNOWN FACT.)

"A little nonsense now and then
Is relished by the wisest men."

Anonymous

Heavenly Waffles

Serves 4-6

Try these with hot applesauce, sausages, & heated maple syrup ~ and ice cold fresh squeezed orange juice. They are quick & easy to make, light & crisp in the new waffle irons that work like a dream — no sticking & easy to clean. ♥

- 2 eggs, beaten
- 1 c. + 2 tbsp. milk
- 3 tbsp. salad oil
- 1½ c. unbleached flour
- 3 tsp. sugar
- 3 tsp. baking powder

Oil waffle iron well, & preheat as per instructions for your iron. In a 3 c. measure, or a bowl with a lip, beat eggs & whisk in milk & salad oil. Stir in flour, sugar, and baking powder to mix, then whisk to get rid of lumps. When iron is hot, pour in batter, carefully, around edges & into middle, just enough to cover. (My iron takes 1 cup.) Close iron quickly to avoid heat loss. Most units now have a light on them that signals when they are done so you won't have to open to check. They bake for about 8 min. & should be very brown & crisp. Melt some butter, heat up maple syrup & serve. ♥

In 1961, my mother was 31, I was 14, and my four brothers ranged in age from about 7 to 13. My mother had just had Shelly, the youngest of the eight. Our yard was where the action was ~ littered with little boy paraphernalia; go-cycles, army equipment, & sports stuff. My mother reigned Queen ~ and it was around this time that the boys, in an attempt to show the great respect & love they had for her, renamed her Mrs. McCurgler. ♥

3 FRUIT SAUCES

DELICIOUS ON WAFFLES, PANCAKES, FRENCH TOAST, GERMAN PANCAKE, & ICE CREAM

MAKES 2 CUPS
- 20 OZ. BAG FROZEN, WHOLE STRAWBERRIES
- 1/2 C. WATER
- 1/2 C. SUGAR

COARSELY CHOP 2/3 OF THE BERRIES – SET ASIDE THE REST. PUT CHOPPED BERRIES, WATER, AND SUGAR IN A STAINLESS S. SAUCEPAN AND BRING TO A BOIL. REDUCE HEAT TO MEDIUM AND CONTINUE TO COOK 15 MIN. STIR IN WHOLE BERRIES AND HEAT THROUGH. SERVE WARM.

MAKES 2 CUPS
- 3 LG. GREEN APPLES (GRANNY SMITH)
- 1 C. WATER
- 1 TBSP. SUGAR
- 1 TSP. CINNAMON

PEEL, CORE, AND COARSELY CHOP APPLES. PUT ALL INGREDIENTS IN A STAINLESS S. SAUCEPAN AND BRING TO A BOIL. REDUCE HEAT TO MEDIUM AND CONTINUE TO COOK 10 MINUTES, STIRRING OFTEN. SERVE WARM.

MAKES 1 1/3 CUPS
- 12 OZ. BAG FROZEN BLUEBERRIES
- 1/3 C. WATER
- 1/3 C. SUGAR
- 1 TSP. GRATED LEMON RIND

PLACE ALL INGREDIENTS IN A STAINLESS S. SAUCEPAN AND BRING TO A BOIL. REDUCE HEAT TO MEDIUM – COOK 5 MIN. GENTLY STRAIN OUT BERRIES AND CONTINUE COOKING LIQUID 5 MORE MIN. (THIS HELPS TO KEEP BERRIES INTACT.) RETURN BERRIES TO JUICE AND HEAT THROUGH. SERVE WARM.

APPLE FRITTERS

Serves 6

Every child's gourmet dream come true! But definitely not for children only. Great at breakfast, delicious for tea, but best of all as a surprise treat – like after playing in the snow, or after school to celebrate the start of Christmas vacation.

4 lg. sweet apples, McIntosh or Cortland
6 c. vegetable oil
1½ c. unbleached flour
⅛ tsp. salt
12 oz. beer, at room temperature
extra flour
½ c. sugar
¾ tsp. cinnamon

Peel, core & slice apples into ½" rings. In a deep pot, heat oil to 350°. Mix together 1½ c. flour, salt & beer; beat well. Put about a cup more of flour into another small bowl. Mix sugar with cinnamon & set aside. Coat apple rings in flour, cover completely with beer batter. Fry in hot oil, a few at a time, for about 4 min. till golden. Drain on paper towels, roll in cinnamon sugar & serve. They can be very hot inside, so be careful!

I heard this on T.V. and thought you'd like a little chuckle while you make these fritters – here goes: "Did you hear they're opening a restaurant on the moon? Great food, but no atmosphere!" Ha Ha Ha :)

CHRISTMAS COFFEE CAKE

350° 9 Servings

Very moist ~ comes out just beautifully. Serve warm from the oven around the tree on Christmas morning.

1 c. flour
1 tsp. soda
½ tsp. salt
1½ c. cored, peeled, chopped apple
1 c. chopped fresh cranberries
1 stick unsalted butter, melted
1 egg, lightly beaten
½ c. light brown sugar
½ c. granulated sugar
¼ tsp. ground cloves
¼ tsp. ground nutmeg
1 tsp. ground cinnamon
½ c. chopped walnuts
powdered sugar, for dusting

Preheat oven to 350°. Sift together flour, soda, & salt ~ set aside. Combine all remaining ingredients & mix well. Stir in flour mixture. Spread in a buttered 8-inch square baking pan. Bake 40-45 min., until knife inserted in center comes out clean. Let sit 10 min., cut into squares, sift over powdered sugar, & serve.

"EVERY TREE THROUGHOUT THE WORLD BLOOMED AND BORE FRUIT ON CHRISTMAS EVE; NATURE SILENTLY, BUT BRILLIANTLY, CELEBRATED THE BIRTH OF CHRIST."

From a Tenth Century legend

SCOTCH EGGS

450° Serves 6

Any ground meat will work for this — I've also used turkey — & they're goooood ♥.

1½ lbs. bulk pork sausage
½ tsp. each: sage, rosemary, & thyme, all crushed } mix together
6 hard-boiled eggs, peeled & chilled
About 1 c. dried bread crumbs

Preheat oven to 450°.

Divide sausage mixture into 6 portions & flatten between palms. Carefully wrap each egg smoothly & completely with sausage; roll in bread crumbs, coating well. Place them 1 in. apart in an ungreased, shallow pan. Bake in top part of oven 30 min., till brown. Drain on paper towels. Serve hot. Delicious with fresh applesauce & buttered toast ♥.

"Thank God for tea! What would the world do without tea? — how did it exist? I am glad I was not born before tea." ♥ Sydney Smith

Oat Bran Muffins

350° Makes 18

First I'll paint this little scene, & then I'll eat it! This is a delicious muffin, moist & tender ~ we gobble them up! They're good for you, & tasty too.

2 c. unbleached flour
1 ½ c. oat bran
1 tsp. baking soda
1 Tbsp. baking powder
2 tsp. cinnamon
½ tsp. nutmeg
grated rind of 1 navel orange
juice of same orange, along with:
about ¾ c. white grape juice (to equal 1 c. juice)
1 c. low-fat buttermilk
½ c. unsulphered molasses
3 egg whites
2 Tbsp. lt. vegetable oil (Puritan)
1 green apple, peeled & diced
½ c. coarse-chopped walnuts
½ c. coarse-chopped dates

Preheat oven to 350°. Lightly oil muffin tins or use paper muffin cups. Thoroughly toss together all dry ingredients in a large bowl. In another bowl, mix together all wet ingredients. Pour liquids into dry & combine, stirring just enough to blend. Fold in apples, walnuts & dates. Fill tins full and bake 10 min. at 350°; turn oven down to 325° & bake 15 min. more.

ORANGE FRENCH TOAST

325° Serves 12

Crisp, not soggy — perfect for a large group since it's all ready at the same time.

- 2 c. fresh orange juice
- 2 c. half & half
- 6 eggs, beaten
- 1/4 c. powdered sugar
- 2 Tbsp. Grand Marnier
- 1 tsp. vanilla extract
- 1 tsp. orange extract
- 2 1-lb. loaves day-old French bread
- 1/2 c. unsalted butter

Preheat oven to 325°. Mix together first 7 ingredients; pour into a lg. shallow dish. Cut bread, diagonally, into 1" slices. Soak bread 2 min. on each side. Brown the slices in butter over med. low heat in a large skillet. When all are browned, place them on cookie sheets (in a single layer) & bake 20 min. Remove from oven, sift over some powdered sugar, & serve hot with heated maple syrup & some orange marmalade. ♥

Cheese Blintzes

Makes 12 Blintzes

Double or triple the crepe recipe – make them ahead & freeze them between sheets of waxed paper; that will make these blintzes a snap to put together later. ♥

Crepes

1 c. whole milk	1 c. unbleached flour
2 eggs, well beaten	1½ Tbsp. butter, melted

Add milk to beaten eggs – whisk in flour, then butter, till smooth. Lightly oil a small (7") skillet – heat pan till moderately hot. Pour about 3 Tbsp. batter into pan & quickly swirl to coat bottom. Brown lightly & turn to cook other side. ♥

Filling

4 oz. cream cheese, softened	1 beaten egg yolk
1 lb. farmers cheese (pot cheese)	1 tsp. vanilla extract
3 Tbsp. powdered sugar	1 tsp. grated lemon juice

Mix together all ingredients until blended, soft & creamy. Place about 3 Tbsp. filling on the lighter side of each crepe & gently fold up sides to make little square packages. You may wrap & refrigerate blintzes for up to 24 hrs. Lightly brown both sides in a small amt. of butter. ♥

To Serve

Place the hot blintzes on serving dishes & pass around small bowls of sour cream, orange marmalade, & raspberry jam. Also wonderful with the delicious fruit sauces on p. 112. ♥

MENU
Christmas Breakfast
Cheese Blintzes
Fruit Sauces
Candied Bacon
&
Good Cheer

Stephen Stewart's Candied Bacon

Serves 6–8

Stephen is the 2nd of my 4 brothers. He used to get me on the ground & press on my eyebrows with the palms of his hands until my eyes almost popped out. I probably deserved it — for all the times I told him how big & strong he was &, so he could joyfully "prove" it, he would pull me up & down the street in the wagon while I hollered "FASTER!" I love that kid & his recipe for Candied Bacon is a knock-out for a holiday breakfast. ♥

1 lb. thick-cut bacon
1/2 c. brown sugar, packed
2 Tbsp. yellow mustard (French's)

Slowly cook bacon in a large skillet till crisp. You will probably have to do this in batches; drain fat each time. Mix together sugar & mustard in a separate bowl. After draining fat for the last time, put all bacon back into pan & set over low heat. Drizzle sugar mixture over bacon, tossing with a fork to coat. Remove immediately & place on serving platter. If slices touch each other, they will stick. Serve. ♥

"THE LITTLE TOY DOG IS COVERED WITH DUST, BUT STURDY AND STAUNCH HE STANDS;
AND THE LITTLE TOY SOLDIER IS COVERED WITH RUST, AND HIS MUSKET MOULDS IN HIS HANDS.
TIME WAS WHEN THE LITTLE TOY DOG WAS NEW, AND THE SOLDIER WAS PASSING FAIR;
AND THAT WAS THE TIME WHEN OUR LITTLE BOY BLUE
KISSED THEM AND PUT THEM THERE."

Eugene Field ♥

EGGS SARDOU CASSEROLE

350° Serves 8

Bacon, eggs & artichoke bottoms on a bed of creamed spinach covered with a rich lemon sauce—perfect for a Christmas breakfast. ♥

2 10 oz. pkgs. creamed spinach, thawed
8 slices bacon, crisply fried, crumbled
8 artichoke bottoms
8 egg yolks
freshly ground pepper, to taste
freshly ground nutmeg, to taste
½ c. plus 2 Tbsp. Parmesan cheese
Lemon Sauce (see below)

NOTE: I want to make this as easy as possible—time is so important, especially during the holidays. But there is no reason, if you are so inclined, that you can't make your own creamed spinach (p. 51) and cook up your own fresh artichokes. ♥ In an 8"×8" baking dish, mix together spinach & crumbled bacon & spread evenly in dish. Press artichoke bottoms into spinach, cup side up & evenly spaced. Gently place an unbroken egg yolk into each artichoke. Sprinkle with pepper, nutmeg & ½ c. Parmesan cheese (grated). Cover all with Lemon Sauce (evenly), then sprinkle over last 2 Tbsp. cheese. Bake 25 min. in a preheated 350° oven. ♥

Lemon Sauce

2 whole eggs
2 egg yolks
1 c. mayonnaise
6 Tbsp. unsalted butter
juice of ½ a juicy lemon
pinch of red pepper flakes, finely crushed

Place all ingredients in double boiler. Whisk over simmering water till thickened. ♥

POTATOES & EGGS

425° Serves 6

Perfect for a midnight supper or a hearty breakfast — these eggs are the creamiest! ♥

3 med. baking potatoes
softened butter
1/3 c. melted butter
salt & pepper

Preheat oven to 425°. Wash, dry, prick the skin & rub each potato with softened butter. Bake 1 hr. Cut them in half lengthwise, remove pulp carefully, leaving a 1/4" shell. Put them on a cookie sheet, brush with melted butter, sprinkle with salt & pepper & return them to oven. Bake 25 min. longer, till shells are crisp & golden. Meanwhile, make the

EGGS

2 Tbsp. butter	1/4 tsp. salt
2 Tbsp. flour	1/8 tsp. white pepper
1/2 c. sour cream	1 bu. green onions, tops only, minced
12 eggs	

In a small pan, over med. heat, melt 1 Tbsp. butter — stir in flour & cook till bubbly. Remove from heat; stir in sour cream. Return to heat, cook till bubbly & smooth. Set aside. Beat together eggs, salt & pepper. In a lg. frying pan over med. heat, melt 1 Tbsp. butter. Pour in eggs, cook gently, stirring often, till eggs are soft set. Remove from heat, stir in sour cream mixture. Fill potato skins with eggs — sprinkle over onion tops & serve. ♥

"Ah friends, dear friends, as
years go on & heads get gray,
how fast the guests do go!
Touch hands, touch hands,
with those that stay.
Strong hands to weak,
old hands to young,
Around the Christmas board
touch hands."

Wm. H. H. Murray

There are so many people who support me while I paint & write — they bring me lunch, fix me dinner, drag me away from my art table & leave me alone. It wouldn't be near as much fun without them♥. So, Christmas Kisses to Joe Hall (kisses all year long to my sweetheart), to my sister, Shelly Stewart, who brought her wonderful sense of humor to me in the NICK of time; to Elaine Sullivan, Margot Datz, Mary Abt &

The love in your heart
wasn't put there to stay,
love isn't love
till it's
given
away.

Valerie Reese — dear friends all.♥ Special thanks to Mary Tondorf-Dick & Edite Kroll for helping me to get my beautiful new house, etc., etc., etc! And of course to my wonderful family & friends out west who call so often to say they're proud of me. And to all you nice people out there who have written or called to say you're enjoying my books — Merry Christmas!

INDEX

Appetizers, ... 9-21
Brie in Puff Pastry, . . 14
Caviar and Oysters, . 12
Chicken Timmies, . . . 20
Chicken Pâté, . . . 19
Christmas Oysters, . . 18
Coconut Shrimp, . 16
Cold Shrimp, ... 10
Heart-Shaped
Cucumber Sandwiches, 17
Lobster Nancy, ... 10
Pesto in Tomatoes, . . 15
Sausage in Brioche, . 11
Smoked Salmon Platter, . 17
Spiced Nuts, . . . 10
Apples
Caramel, . 93
Fritters, . . . 113
Sauce, . . . 112
and Wild Rice, . . . 41
Apricots, Dried, . . 50

Bacon, Stephen
Stewart's Candied, . . 119
Beef
Roast Prime Ribs of, . . 74
Whiskey Steaks, ... 75
Beverages, . . . 26–33
cold
Angel Tea, . . . 26
Classic Egg Nog, . . . 30
Iced Vodka with
Sweetheart Roses, . 27
Mint Julep, . . . 26
Peach Cream, . . 31
Sober Water, . . . 32
hot
Chocolate Mint . . . 26
Chocolate Mint Coffee, 29
Coffee Grog, . . . 32
Elfin Wine, . . . 33
Hot Buttered Rum, . . 26
Spiced Cider, ... 28
Blintzes, Cheese, ... 118
Blueberry Sauce, . . . 112
Breakfast & Brunch, 111–121
Apple Fritters, . . 113
Candied Bacon, . . . 119
Cheese Blintzes, ... 118
Christmas Coffee Cake, . 114
Eggs Sardou Casserole, . 120
Heavenly Waffles, . . . 111
Oat Bran Muffins, . . 116
Orange French Toast, . . 117
Potatoes & Eggs, ... 121
Scotch Eggs, ... 115
Brioche, Sausage in, . . . 11

Cake, Christmas Coffee, . 114
Candles, decorating with, 22-23
Candy
Caramel apples, . . . 93
Popcorn Balls, . . . 93
Rum Truffles, . . . 92
Caroling, ... 60
Carrots in Orange-
Ginger Sauce, ... 46
Casseroles
Eggs Sardou, . . . 120
Sweet Potato with
Walnuts, ... 49
Turkey Lasagna, . . . 70
Wild Rice & Apples, . 41
Caviar & Oysters, . . . 12
Cheese
Blintzes, ... 118
Brie, in Puff Pastry, . . 14
Cherries Jubilee, . . . 103
Chicken
appetizers, ... 19, 20
Cranberry Chicken
& Pears, ... 69
Timmies, ... 20
Pâté, ... 19
Children
and Santa Claus, . 76–77
celebrating Christmas
with, ... 37
Chocolate
Chocolate Dipped Coconut
Macaroons, ... 89
Croquembouche, . . 96
Mary's Mother's
Snowballs, ... 85
Mint (beverage), . . 26
Mint Coffee, ... 29
Poached Pears, . . . 94
Pots de Crème, . . . 95
Sauce, ... 94
Christmas cards
as decorations, . . 22
ideas for
child's drawing, . . . 57
postcards, ... 34
postmark on, ... 77
Christmas Day activities, 62
Christmas Eve Dinner
Feast, ... 72

Cider, Spiced, . . . 23
Coconut
Chocolate Dipped Coconut Macaroons, ... 89
Shrimp, ... 16
Coffee
Cake, Christmas, ... 114
Chocolate Mint, ... 29
Grog, ... 32
Collections, ideas for, . . 104
Cookies
Annie Hall's Butter, 82-83
Candy Canes, ... 83
Chocolate Dipped Coconut Macaroons, ... 89
Christmas Nut, . . . 88
Christmas Wreaths, . . 84
Cookie Cutter, ... 83
Fairy Cones, ... 13
Florentine, ... 90
as gifts, ... 81
Grandma's Frosted Molasses, ... 86
Jelly-Filled, ... 83
Lemon Squares, . . . 101
Mary's Mother's Snowballs, ... 85
Plain Old Drop, . . 83
Roll, ... 83
Snowflakes, ... 87
Cranberry Chicken & Pears, ... 69
Crepes, ... 118
Croquembouche, ... 96
Croutons, Star, . . . 15, 38
Cucumber Sandwiches, Heart-Shaped, ... 17
Custard
Bourbon, ... 99
Vanilla, ... 97
Decorating ideas, . . . 22-23
Baked Christmas Decorations, ... 105
balloons, ... 37
for children, ... 37
Cinnamon Spice, . . . 61
Fragrant Herb Bundles, 61
Sugared Fruit, ... 22
Teddy Bear Tea Party, ... 108
Yule Log, ... 61
Doggie Treats, ... 21
Drinks. See Beverages
Egg Nog, Classic, ... 30
Eggs
and Potatoes, ... 121
Sandou Casserole, . . . 120
Scotch, ... 115
Fish. See Seafood
Flowers, ... 22, 37
French Toast, Orange, . . . 117
Fritters, Apple, ... 113
Frosting, ... 86
Fruit dishes
apples
Apple Fritters, ... 113
Apple Sauce, ... 112
Caramel Apples, . . . 93
Wild Rice & Apples, . 41
apricots, ... 50
Cherries Jubilee, . . . 103
Lemon Squares, . . . 101
oranges
Candied Orange Peel, ... 91
Carrots in Orange-Ginger Sauce, . . . 46
Orange French Toast, ... 117
Orange Sauce, . . . 65
Orange Watercress Salad, ... 47
Sliced Oranges, . . 50
pears
Chocolate Poached Pears, ... 94
Cranberry Chicken & Pears, ... 69
sauces, ... 65, 112
Fruit salads
Christmas Eve, . . . 43
Fresh Fruit, ... 52
Orange Watercress, . . 47
Gift ideas
for children, ... 37
collections, ... 104
cookies, ... 81
Doggie Treats, ... 21
Fragrant Herb Bundles, 61
hobbies as, . . 38, 58, 104
hostess gifts, ... 38
for newlyweds, . . . 57
photos, ... 57
serenade, ... 57
Star Croutons, ... 15
Stocking Stuffers, . . 58
Ginger
Carrots in Orange-Ginger Sauce, . . . 46
and Lime Sauce, . . . 73
Squash, ... 45
Goose, Mother's, . . 64, 65
Gravy, turkey, ... 55

Ham, Honey, ... 71
Horseradish Sauce, . . . 74
Hostess Gifts, ... 38

Lamb, Mustard
Roasted Leg of, . . . 68
Lasagna, Turkey, ... 70
Lemon Squares, ... 101
Lime & Ginger Sauce, . 73
Lobster
Nancy, ... 10
Steamed, ... 72
Luminarias, ... 23

Macaroons, Chocolate
Dipped Coconut, . . . 89
Main Dishes, ... 63~75
Cranberry Chicken
& Pears, ... 69
Honey Ham, ... 71
Mother's Goose, . . 64~65
Mustard Roasted
Leg of Lamb, ... 68
Poached Salmon with
Lime & Ginger Sauce, 73
Roast Prime Ribs
of Beef, ... 74
Roast Turkey, . . 66~67
Steamed Lobsters, . . . 72
Turkey Lasagna, . . . 70
Whiskey Steaks, . . . 75
Meringue, in Snow Clouds, 99
Mint
Chocolate Mint
Beverage, ... 26
Chocolate Mint
Coffee, ... 29
Julep, ... 26
Peas, ... 40
Muffins, Oat Bran, . . . 116
Mustard Roasted Leg
of Lamb, ... 68

Nuts
Christmas Nut
Cookies, ... 88
Hot Almond Crunch, . 92
Spiced, ... 10
in Sweet Potato
Casserole, ... 49

Oat Bran Muffins, . . 116
Onions, Creamed, . . . 48
Oranges
Candied Orange Peel, 91
Carrots in Orange~
Ginger Sauce, . . . 46
Orange French Toast, 117
Orange Watercress
Salad, ... 47
Sauce, ... 65
Sliced, ... 50
Oysters
as appetizers, . . . 12, 18
and Caviar, ... 12
Christmas, ... 18

Party ideas
caroling, ... 60
champagne, ... 12
for children, . . 37, 108
Teddy Bear Tea, . . 108
Pastry
Brie in, ... 14
Croquembouche, . . . 96
puff, ... 14, 96
Pâté, Chicken, ... 19
Peach Cream, ... 31
Pears
Chocolate Poached, . . . 94
Cranberry Chicken &, . 69
Peas, Minty, ... 40
Pecans, Spiced, ... 10
Pesto in Tomatoes, . . . 15
Popcorn Balls, ... 93
Potatoes
and Eggs, ... 121
Sweet Potato Casserole
with Walnuts, . . . 49
Poultry
Cranberry Chicken
& Pears, ... 69
Mother's Goose, . . 64~65
Roast Turkey, . . 66~67
Turkey Lasagna, . . . 70
Pudding
Crème de Pumpkin, . . 100
Father's Bread Pudding
with Whiskey Sauce, . 98
Pots de Crème, ... 95
Snow Clouds, . . . 99
Steamed Christmas, . 102
Tipsy Trifle, ... 97
Vanilla Custard, . . 98
Yorkshire, ... 74
Puff pastry, ... 14, 96
Pumpkin, Crème de, . . 100

Rice, Wild, & Apples, . 41

Salads
Christmas Eve, . . . 43
Fresh Fruit, ... 52
Orange Watercress, . . 47
Warm Spinach, . . . 53

Salmon
Poached, with Lime & Ginger Sauce, . . . 73
Smoked, Platter, ... 17
Sandwiches
Cucumber, ... 17
Smoked Salmon, . . . 17
Santa Claus, ... 76-77
Sauces
Caramel, ... 99
Chocolate, ... 94, 96
Fruit, ... 112
Hard, ... 102
Horseradish, ... 74
Hot Almond Crunch, . . 92
Lime & Ginger, ... 73
Orange, ... 65
Orange-Ginger, . . . 46
Whiskey, ... 98
Seafood
Caviar & Oysters, . . . 12
Christmas Oysters, . . 18
Coconut Shrimp, . . . 16
Cold Shrimp, ... 10
Lobster Nancy, ... 10
Poached Salmon, . . . 73
Smoked Salmon Platter, 17
Steamed Lobster, ... 72
Shallots, Roasted, . . . 42
Shrimp
Coconut, ... 16
Cold, ... 10
Snow, ... 34, 35
soap, ... 34
Cones, ... 34
games, ... 34
Spinach
Creamed, ... 51
Warm, Salad, . . . 53
Squash, Ginger, ... 45
Stocking Stuffers, . . . 58
Strawberry Sauce, . . . 112
Stuffing
Turkey, ... 54
Wild Rice & Apples, . 41
Superstitions, ... 110
Sweet Potato Casserole with Walnuts, . . . 49
Toys
as decorations, . . . 23, 108
as stocking stuffers, . . 58
Trees, Christmas, . . 22, 36
Trifle, Tipsy, ... 97
Truffles, Rum, ... 92
Turkey
Gravy, ... 55
Lasagna, ... 70
Roast, ... 66-67
Stuffing 41, 54
Vanilla Custard, . . . 97
Vegetables
Carrots in Orange-Ginger Sauce, . . . 46
Creamed Onions, . . . 48
Creamed Spinach, . . . 51
Ginger Squash, . . . 45
Minty Peas, ... 40
mixed, Sauté, ... 44
Roasted Shallots, . . . 42
Sweet Potato Casserole, 49
Warm Spinach Salad, 53
Vodka, Iced, with Sweetheart Roses, . . . 27
Waffles, Heavenly, . . . 111
Watercress, in salad, . . 47
Yorkshire Pudding, . . 74
Yule Logs, ... 61

P.S. My other books, Heart of the Home & Vineyard Seasons, have delicious recipes for Christmas — here are a few:

Appetizers
Clams Casino, . . . 18H
Cream Cheese & Pesto Mold, . . . 23H
Stuffed French Bread, 24H
Beverages
Champagne Cocktails, 114H
Witches Brew, . . . 136V
Breakfast & Tea
Apple Muffins . . 146V
German Pancake, . 147H
Maple Pecan Scones, . . . 147V
Nut Bread, . . . 149V
Popovers, ... 149H
Main Dishes
Chicken in Cherry Sauce, . . . 105V
Roast Wild Duck Glaze, ... 102H
Cornish Game Hens, 104H
Salads
Orange & Onion, . 50V
Rainbow Jello, . . 62H
Desserts & Candy
Bourbon Balls, . 134V
Chocolate Mousse, . 140V
Snowball in Hell, . 146V
and many more . . .